Safety Note

This book is all about having fun while learning new outdoor skills. You should always ask an adult before beginning any of the featured activities. Ask an adult to work with you when foraging, cooking, building a fire or using any of the tools featured in the book. Be certain to let an adult know when you are going outdoors for any activity.

MAGIC CAT PUBLISHING

The Handbook of Forgotten Skills Outdoors © 2026 Lucky Cat Publishing Ltd
Text © 2026 Iron Tazz
Illustrations © 2026 Deborah Hocking
First Published in 2026 by Magic Cat Publishing, an imprint of Lucky Cat Publishing Ltd,
Unit 2 Empress Works, 24 Grove Passage, London E2 9FQ, UK
EU Authorised Representative Magic Cat Publishing, an imprint of Lucky Cat Publishing Ltd,
PAKTA svetovanje d.o.o., Stegne 33, Ljubljana, Slovenia

A catalogue record for this book is available from the British Library.

ISBN 978-1-917044-80-6

The illustrations in this book were created using watercolour, monotype, printmaking and digital.
Set in Edith, Kalam, Nature Spirit, Recoleta and Wisely.

Published by Rachel Williams and Jenny Broom
Designed by Ashtyn Botterill
Edited by Mary Jones and Rachel Williams

Manufactured in China
1 3 5 7 9 8 6 4 2

The HANDBOOK of forgotten skills ...OUTDOORS

written by IRON TAZZ
illustrated by DEBORAH HOCKING

MAGIC CAT PUBLISHING

Have you ever wondered what life was like before Wi-Fi, tablets or video games? Your great-grandparents didn't need smartphones or the Internet to have fun. They hiked, built, cooked and created – learning outdoor skills that made every day an adventure!

You can't hop in a time machine, but you can step outside. Learn to use a compass, tie a knot, catch a fish or cook over a campfire. Explore the world beyond the walls. Build something useful, or just something fun! You'll be surprised by how much you can do – and how good it feels to make things on your own.

The skills in this book may have been forgotten, but they're just waiting for someone like you to discover them . . .

THIS BOOK WAS MADE BY:

Iron Tazz is an avid camper, backpacker, hiker and artist, who wrote the text for this book. After spending more than 400 nights under the stars and 16,000 kilometres on the trail, he is committed to teaching others the skills they need to be prepared and connected in the wild and to inspiring families to explore nature together. He is the author of *Hike It: An Introduction to Camping, Hiking, and Backpacking in the U.S.A.*

Website: irontazz.com
TikTok: @hike.it
Youtube: @Hike-it
Instagram: @iron.tazz

Deborah Hocking is a creator based in the US Pacific Northwest. She is the author-illustrator of the nonfiction picture book *The Great Pollination Investigation* and the illustrator of the chapter book series, Sydney & Taylor. Deborah finds her greatest inspiration while hiking and camping, immersed in the landscapes she draws. She sketched the first drafts of the illustrations for *The Handbook of Forgotten Skills: Outdoors* from her truck camper dinette table while exploring Baja, Mexico, and the Western United States.

Website: deborahhockingstudio.com
Instagram: @deborahhockingstudio

CONTENTS

A BUSHCRAFTER'S TOOLBOX

Some toolboxes don't sit in a garage or have metal drawers – they strap right onto your back. Your rucksack is your toolbox, packed with just the right equipment to help you explore, build and thrive in the wild – skills we call bushcraft. Every item has a job to do, from starting a fire to staying dry when the rain hits. Long ago, people and communities thrived, relying on just a few tools and clever thinking. Now it's your turn to keep the adventure alive!

Essential Tools Checklist

There are legends who survive the wild with nothing but a knife and grit. While that's super impressive, most people prefer thriving over surviving.

Here are the core tools that everyone should include in their kit:

Making Smart Equipment Choices

Choosing equipment for the wild is all about balance: You want enough to stay safe and thrive, but not so much that it weighs you down. The trick is to focus on essentials, and picking tools that are multipurpose, lightweight and durable.

Tools You Might Add to Your Core Kit:

- Hatchet or axe
- Foldable saw
- Multi-tool
- Fishing kit
- Stove

Don't depend on fire

You might misplace your fire starter, or the conditions may be so wet that starting one is impossible. A water filter is a must (since you can't boil water without fire), and carrying a solid shelter and sleep setup is key to staying cosy and dry, no matter what comes your way!

Sleeping comfortably

Don't skip the sleeping mat! Your sleeping bag isn't enough by itself – the ground pulls heat fast. A foam mat or compact air mattress helps keep you warm and comfy.

A −8°C sleeping bag (comfortable to temperatures as low as −8°C) is a solid all-round choice for most environments. Choose one with synthetic filling or treated down, as they'll still insulate even when damp.

Tarp or tent

Tarps are lighter than tents, pack down small and can be turned into all kinds of creative shelters. Tents are great too – offering full coverage and protection from insects.

Protective Clothing

Rain or shine, it's all fine – if your equipment's in line. Pack these essentials:

Cold weather clothes: a warm layer like a wool jumper or down jacket

Wool or synthetic base layers (they insulate even when wet)

Sun protection: sunglasses, sunscreen, hat

What to Look for in a Rucksack

- A good fit for your body
- Comfortable to wear, even when fully loaded
- Enough capacity to carry all tools, clothing and food

Tip: Line the inside of your rucksack with a large rubbish bag to keep your equipment dry.

PURIFY WILD WATER

Drinking straight from a crystal-clear stream might seem tempting but don't be fooled – nasty bacteria, viruses and parasites like Giardiasis might be lurking. They can turn your camping trip into a bathroom-bound nightmare! Thankfully, you've got options. Boiling water is the gold standard. Even the most hardened explorers rely on this method. But if boiling isn't possible, a trusty water filter, purifying tablets or a UV light purifier can save the day.

Different Methods for Purifying Water

Whether it's a stream, lake, river or pond, wild water needs treatment before drinking. There are a few ways to do it, and each method has its pros and cons, so the best choice depends on your situation. Many outdoor explorers use a combination, like filtering first and then using chemical drops or UV light for extra protection.

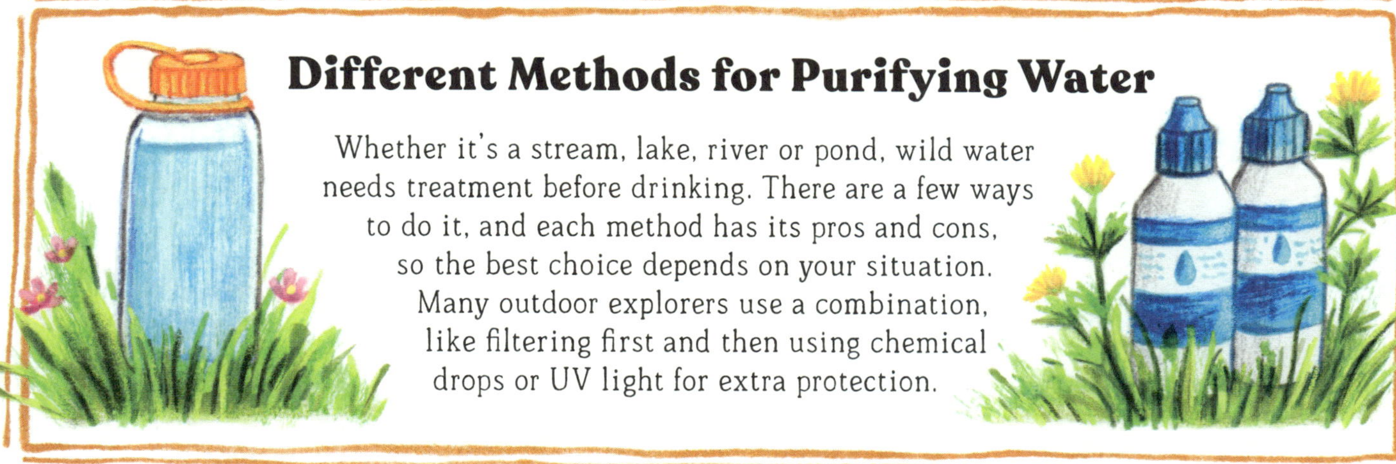

Boiling is one of the most reliable methods. Bring water to a rolling boil for at least one minute (three minutes at higher elevations) to kill bacteria, viruses and parasites. A metal canteen or cooking pot is your best container.

Solar disinfection (SODIS), where clear bottles of water are placed in direct sunlight for six hours, can kill harmful organisms, but it's not the fastest or most reliable method.

Purification tablets/drops use chemical treatments like iodine or chlorine dioxide to kill most pathogens. They're lightweight and easy to use but can leave a slight taste.

UV purification uses UV light to zap harmful microorganisms, making water safe in seconds. They're battery-operated and work best in clear water.

Filtration uses fine membranes to remove bacteria, protozoa and debris. Some even remove viruses, but most do not. If you can, find a portable filter that attaches straight to a water bottle or bladder.

How to Make a DIY Survival Water Filter
This method mimics nature's filtration process and can be a lifesaver in the wild.
What you need:
- An empty plastic bottle (or similar container)
- A knife or scissors
- Charcoal (from a fire)
- Sand
- Small gravel or pebbles
- A piece of cloth, bandana or coffee filter
- Dirty or cloudy water
- A pot or bottle to collect filtered water
- String
String
Bottle
Dirty water
Gravel
Sand
Charcoal
Cloth
Cup
Step 1: Cut the Bottle
→ Cut the bottom off a plastic bottle about 3–5 centimetres from the bottom. This will be your open end for adding materials.
Step 2: Create a Drainage Hole
→ Carefully poke a small hole in the bottle cap to allow filtered water to drip through. If you don't have a cap, tie a piece of cloth over the bottle's opening.

Step 3: *Layer the Filter Materials (from Bottom to Top)*

→ ***Cloth or Bandana**: Place a piece of cloth inside the bottle opening to prevent materials from falling through.*

→ ***Charcoal Layer**: Crush charcoal into small pieces and add a layer at least 5 centimetres thick. Charcoal removes toxins and chemicals, and improves taste.*

→ ***Sand Layer**: Add a layer of fine sand (about 5 centimetres thick). This helps trap smaller debris and sediments.*

→ ***Gravel or Small Pebbles**: Place a layer of gravel or small rocks on top (another 5 centimetres), to help catch large debris before it reaches the sand.*

Step 4: *Hang the Bottle*

→ *Tie a piece of paracord or string to your bottle so you can hang it on a branch or wooden tripod (filtering can be a slow process).*

Step 5: *Pour Water Through*

→ *Slowly pour dirty water into the top of the filter and let it trickle through all the layers. Collect the filtered water in a clean container at the bottom (this could be your metal pot or bottle used for boiling).*

Step 6: *Repeat & Purify*

→ *Run the water through the filter at least twice for better results.*

Important: This filter removes dirt and some contaminants, but it does not kill bacteria or viruses. For safe drinking water, always boil, use purification tablets or apply UV light after filtering.

SET UP CAMP

Setting up camp is more than just survival – it's about creating a cosy home in the wild. Every detail, from where you lay your head to how you build your fire, connects you to the land. Indigenous peoples, like the Ojibwe of the northern United States and southern Canada, mastered campcraft. They used deep knowledge of the land to live in harmony with nature. Whether you're pitching a tent or crafting a lean-to, it's an opportunity to slow down, work with the earth and truly experience the magic of the great outdoors.

Camp Checklist

Scout the area

Don't just drop your gear and settle – take a few minutes to explore! A 'good-enough' spot might work, but the perfect campsite could be just a short walk away.

Clear & prep the site

Remove rocks, sticks and debris for a comfortable setup.

Set up shelter

Pitch your tent or build a shelter with natural materials.

Build a fire pit

Choose a safe spot, gather dry wood and create a fire ring. Always best to use an existing fire pit if possible.

Organize your camp

Keep sleeping, cooking, and food storage areas separate for safety.

Stay comfortable

Arrange equipment, adjust for wind and shade and set up a cosy sleep system.

Leave no trace

Pack out what you pack in, minimize impact and respect nature. The goal? Leave the spot looking like you were never there – so nature stays wild for the next explorer.

Settle in & enjoy

Relax, watch the fire, soak in the stars and enjoy the adventure!

Pick Your Campsite

When picking a spot, always remember the Four W's: Wind, Water, Wood and Wildlife – each one is key to keeping you safe, comfortable and connected to nature.

Wood

If you're planning a campfire, set up near fallen, dry wood – never strip live trees. Finding a spot close to firewood is preferable to carrying it long distances to camp.

Water

Camp near a water source, but try to stay at least 60 metres away to protect the ecosystem. Avoid setting up in depressions (low points that can fill with rainwater).

Wind

Look for tree clusters, hills or boulders that block the wind. Make sure there are no dead branches above your spot, or dead trees next to it. These dangers are often known as 'widow-makers'.

Wildlife

Be mindful of animal trails, nests or signs of large predators. Cook and store food away from camp so you don't attract curious creatures.

Minimize Impact

Use existing campsites if possible. This helps protect untouched wilderness. That said, there are plenty of existing sites with widow-makers overhead or situated in low points that could flood with water – avoid those!

Going to the loo outdoors

We all go to the loo. If you're out hiking or camping there might not be a toilet nearby! Here's the Leave No Trace method.

Step 1: ***Find the Right Spot & Dig a Cathole***

→ *Walk at least 60 metres (70 big steps) away from water, trails and campsites.*

→ *Look for soft soil to dig in and a private area with some natural cover.*

→ *Use a trowel, stick, walking pole or boot heel to dig a cathole 15–20 centimetres deep (about the length of your hand).*

Step 2: ***Do Your Business & Wipe Properly***

→ *Squat over the hole. (If squatting is tough, dig your cathole near a 'toilet tree' that you can lean against.)*

→ *When you're done, wipe using toilet paper or natural alternatives like smooth stones, leaves (that aren't poisonous!) or snow.*

→ *Collect all toilet paper in a sealable bag.*

Step 3: ***Cover & Disguise***

→ *Fill in the hole with the original soil and natural debris like leaves or sticks.*

→ *If possible, put two sticks crossed in an X on top to signal to the next person NOT to dig here.*

Step 4: ***Sanitise***

→ *Use hand sanitiser to clean your hands.*

Wag Bags

In some sensitive areas such as deserts, alpine zones or popular trails, it's a rule to collect your waste using a wag bag (a special waste bag with absorbent gel). Fun!

BUILD A NATURAL SHELTER

Long before tarps and tents, people built shelters from what the land gave them – branches, bark, leaves and even snow. The Sami, one of Europe's oldest Indigenous groups, built warm, windproof structures from bent saplings and reindeer hides to survive the Arctic cold. Learning to build with natural materials trains your eye, sharpens your instincts and turns the wild into your own epic fort!

Different Styles of Natural Shelters

There are endless ways to build a shelter in the wild, but these time-tested styles are some of the most practical and reliable for real-life survival.

A-frame – a classic triangle shape, like a tent. Rest a long stick (the ridge pole) on the ground or a forked support. Lean strong sticks evenly along both sides and cover them thickly with debris. A solid choice for rainy days, wind or cool nights.

Debris hut – a low, snug structure built like a mini A-frame, sealed with thick layers of leaves, grass and moss. Crawl in feet-first. Best when it's cold and you don't want to rely on a fire.

Lean-to – lash a ridge pole between two trees, then lean strong sticks against it. Cover with leaves, bark or pine boughs. Quick to build, it's great for mild weather and it can reflect heat from a campfire.

Snow cave – hollowed straight into a snowbank. Dig a tunnel and raised sleeping area inside. Windproof and surprisingly warm, it's perfect for deep winter conditions. They're also fun to build.

Log cabin style – stack branches or logs in a square to form walls, then build a roof with more wood and forest debris. Takes effort, and lots of wood, but offers strong protection and a semi-permanent shelter.

Nature's Building Kit

How to Build a Natural A-Frame Shelter

The A-frame is one of the best all-around shelters. It's simple to build, easy to insulate and solid in almost any weather.

Step 1: ***Set the Ridge Pole.*** *Find a long, sturdy branch or a small log a touch longer than your height. Prop one end between two forked sticks or a low tree crotch and the other on the ground. Paracord can help you secure your ridge pole.*

Step 2: ***Build the Frame.*** *Lean strong sticks along both sides of the ridge pole, creating a triangle shape.*

Step 3: ***Add Smaller Sticks.*** *Fill in the gaps by leaning smaller branches over the main frame. The tighter the better – it holds your cover in place.*

Step 4: ***Cover with Debris.*** *Pile on leaves, grass, pine needles or bark. Start from the bottom and layer upward, like shingles. Go thick – at least 30 centimetres deep if you can!*

Step 5: ***Make a Bushcraft Mattress.*** *Lay down a thick bed of leaves, pine boughs or grass inside the shelter. This insulates you from the cold ground.*

Step 6: ***Test and Adjust.*** *Climb in! If you feel wind or see light coming through, patch it up with more debris.*

Master the Four S's of Shelter Building

Scout smart

Look for flat, dry ground near trees, rocks or hills that can block wind. The best shelters start by picking the right spot – that way, half the work is already done for you.

Solid first – soft later

Build a strong frame before adding leaves or branches. Give it a few good pushes to test it – if it wobbles, it's not ready.

Stay dry – pile high

Use debris like leaves, moss and bark to trap warmth and block wind. More layers mean better insulation.

Small opening – big difference

Face the entrance away from the wind and keep it low. A small opening holds in body heat and keeps out cold and rain.

BUILD A CAMPFIRE

Fire changed everything. When our early ancestors first sparked a flame, it gave them warmth, safety and the power to cook – fuelling brain growth and shaping human evolution. Campfires became places for stories, connection and survival. So, next time you're roasting marshmallows, stargazing or laughing with your best friend by the fire, remember, you're carrying on a tradition as old as humanity itself.

Methods for Lighting a Fire

Matches

Simple and dependable. Keep them dry. Waterproof matches or a waterproof case is best.

Firesteel

A bushcraft essential! Scrape the rod with a steel striker to throw super-hot sparks that can ignite tinder. It takes practice, but works in tough conditions.

Advanced methods

For those ready to level up – try flint and steel, a bow drill or even a magnifying glass on a sunny day. These take skill, but are great backups if your main methods fail.

Lighter

Quick and easy, but not foolproof. Wind, cold or running out of fuel can all cause problems.

Tip:

Ask an adult to help you practise using your firesteel, and ALWAYS carry backups like waterproof matches and a lighter – just in case.

A Step-by-Step Guide to Building a Campfire

Step 1: ***Choose a Safe Spot.*** *Pick a clear area away from shelters, trees, dry grass or anything flammable. Use a fire ring if there is one, or make a circle of rocks to keep things contained.*

Step 2: ***Gather Your Materials.***

Remember: *Protect the ecosystem and use dead, fallen wood. Never strip live trees.*

You'll need three types of fuel:

- ***Tinder:*** *Dry, fluffy stuff like dry grass, bark or wood shavings.*

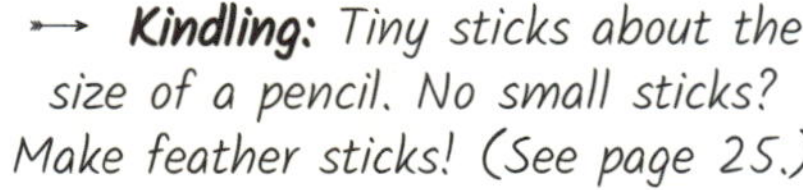

- ***Kindling:*** *Tiny sticks about the size of a pencil. No small sticks? Make feather sticks!* *(See page 25.)*
- ***Fuel wood:*** *Bigger sticks and logs to keep your fire going.*

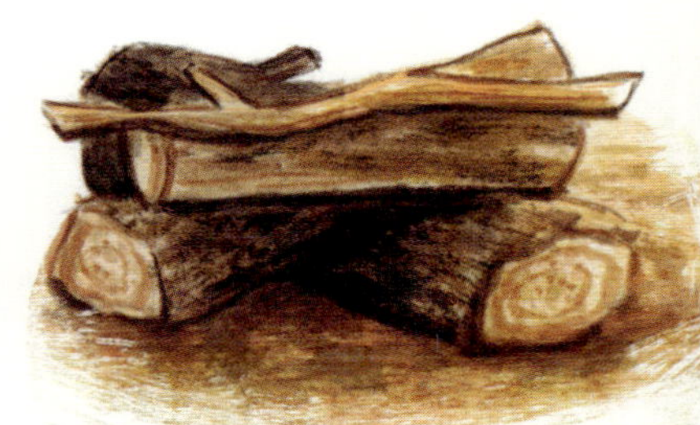

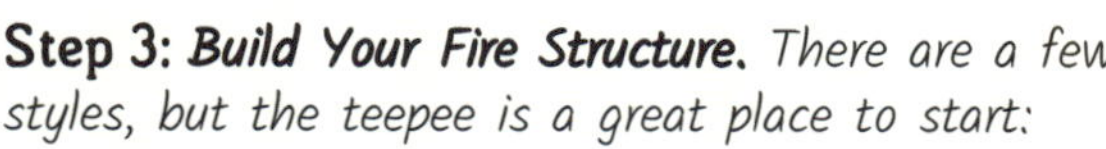

Step 3: ***Build Your Fire Structure.*** *There are a few styles, but the teepee is a great place to start:*

- *Put a small pile of tinder in the centre.*

- *Lean kindling sticks around the tinder like a teepee.*

- *Add some slightly larger sticks on the outside – but not too many yet! Your fire needs air.*

Step 4: ***Light the Fire.*** *Use your chosen method (firesteel, matches or lighter) to light the tinder at the base. Gently blow to help the flames grow if needed.*

Step 5: ***Feed the Fire.*** *As the kindling catches, add more small sticks, then slowly add your fuel wood. Don't smother it! Fires love air just as much as fuel.*

Tip: *Prep extra kindling and small sticks before lighting your fire. If your flames die before the big wood catches, you'll have to start over.*

Essential Fire Safety

- Check for fire bans before heading out.
- Keep it small – build only as big a fire as you need.
- Never leave a fire unattended.
- Have water nearby, just in case.
- Never build a fire ring with wet river rocks – they can explode when heated.
- Make sure your fire is 100% extinguished before leaving.

How to Properly Extinguish a Campfire

Step 1: ***Cool It Down.*** *Let the fire burn down. Then, spread out the embers with a stick.*

Step 2: ***Add Water.*** *Pour water over the fire, making sure to get all the hot spots.*

Listen for the sizzling sound – it's telling you where there's still heat!

Step 3: ***Stir It Up.*** *Use a stick to stir the wet ashes and embers. You might still hear some crackling – keep stirring and adding water, if so.*

Step 4: ***Feel for Heat.*** *Carefully hover your hand above the ashes. If you feel heat, add more water and stir again.*

Step 5: ***Double-check.*** *When you're sure the fire is completely out, give everything one last look. There should be no smoke, no heat – just cool, wet ashes.*

Now, you're good to go! Remember, a safe fire is a completely put-out fire.

DIY Fire Starters: Step-by-Step Guide

Carrying a homemade fire starter means you've got a reliable way to spark a fire fast, even if the wood is damp or the weather's not on your side.

How to Make 'Flame Pods'

What you need:

- Empty cardboard egg carton
- Dryer lint (from your washing)
- Wax (old candles or crayon bits work well)
- Empty, clean tin can
- Pot and something to stir with
- Oven mitt

No dryer at home? Substitute lint for small wood chips.

Step 1: ***Fill the Cups.*** *Stuff each egg cup with dryer lint. Press it down a bit, but not too tight.*

Step 2: ***Melt the Wax.*** *Place your wax in a tin can. With an adult's help, place the can in a pot with some water over low heat to melt the wax. Stir occasionally. Be careful – it gets hot!*

Step 3: ***Pour It In.*** *Give the melted wax a stir. Then, using an oven glove, carefully pour wax into each cup to cover the lint. Let it soak in.*

Step 4: ***Let It Cool.*** *Leave the egg carton to cool and harden. This usually takes about an hour.*

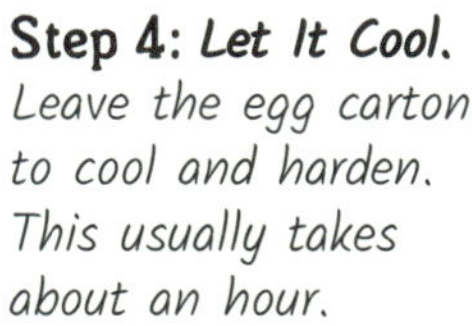

Step 5: ***Break & Pack.*** *Tear or cut each cup apart, and just like that, you've got 12 ready-to-go fire starters!*

Tip:

Throw a couple in a resealable bag, and keep them in your bushcrafter's toolbox.

WHITTLE WOOD

For centuries, whittling has been a vital skill for survival and creativity. Pioneers, hunters and outdoor explorers used it to craft tools, repair equipment and shape the world around them. In bushcraft, whittling is more than just carving. It's a hands-on way to connect with nature and build self-reliance. Tent stakes, feather sticks or a sturdy spoon – each project sharpens patience, craftsmanship and problem-solving. With just a sharp knife and the right technique, whittling empowers adventurers to create, adapt and thrive in the wild.

Useful Things You Can Whittle

Tent stakes

Secure your shelter with strong, custom-made stakes.

Pot hook

Use a hooked branch to hang pots over the fire. You can even make this with adjustable heights.

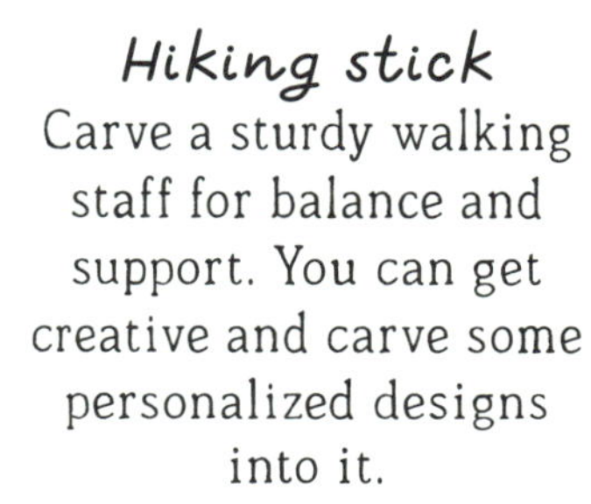

Hiking stick

Carve a sturdy walking staff for balance and support. You can get creative and carve some personalized designs into it.

Spoon

Whittle a basic but essential eating utensil.

Fire bow drill set

Make a spindle, bow and fire board to start a fire.

Whistle

Create a survival whistle for signalling.

Fishing spear

Sharpen a multi-pronged spear for catching fish.

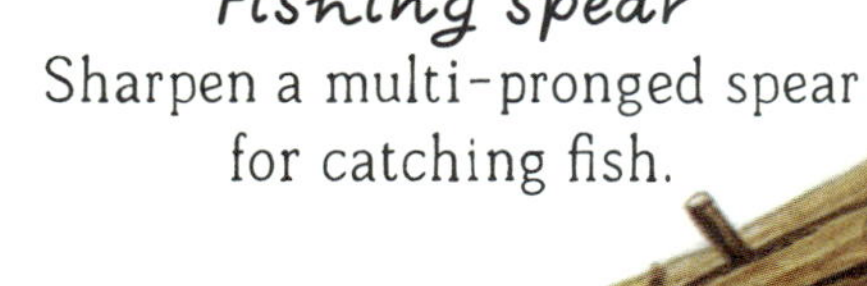

Feather stick

(sometimes called a fuzz stick) Carefully shave a piece of wood to create curls that remain attached to the stick. An essential fire starter.

Cooking spit

Sharpen a stick and support it over a fire for roasting meat or vegetables.

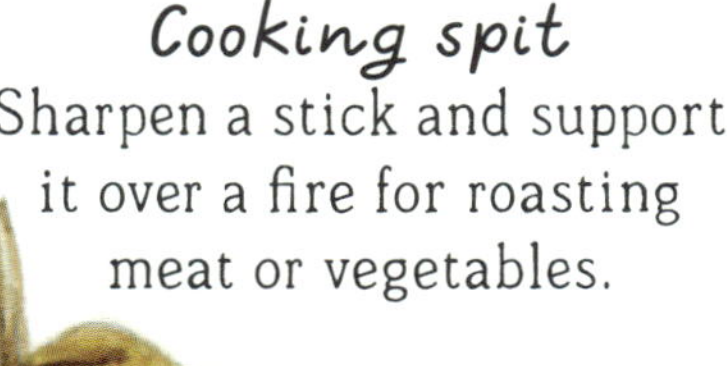

A Few Words on Knife Safety

Sharpness matters
A sharp knife is safer than a dull one. It requires less force, reducing the chance of slipping.

Firm grip
Hold the knife firmly with a grip that gives you control. Don't grip too tightly, but maintain a secure hold.

Keep fingers clear
Always keep your fingers out of the path of the blade. Curl your fingers on your non-dominant hand to protect them.

Cut away from yourself
Whenever possible, cut away from your body, not towards it.

Elbows on knees
NEVER whittle on your legs or lap. Keep your elbows on your knees and carve in front of you.

Control the blade
Use smooth, controlled strokes. Don't rush or force the knife.

Sheathing
When not in use, store your knife in a sheath. This protects the blade and prevents accidental injuries.

Finding the Right Knife for the Outdoors

A good knife is arguably the most valuable tool in your kit. Ask an adult to help you choose a knife and get comfortable using it safely. When picking one, look for these features.

Fixed blade
A fixed blade offers superior strength and reliability compared to folding knives.

Quality steel
High-carbon steels are tough and hold an edge well, but they can be prone to rust. Stainless steels are more corrosion-resistant and more suitable for wet conditions.

Full tang
A full tang, where the blade steel extends through the entire length of the handle, is considered the strongest and most reliable option.

Ergonomic design
A comfortable and secure grip is essential. The handle should allow for extended use without causing discomfort.

Optimal length
A blade length of around 9–13 centimetres is ideal for chopping, batoning and fine tasks like whittling.

Protective sheath
A quality sheath is essential for carrying and protecting your knife. It should be durable, secure and allow for easy access to the knife.

Whittle a Spoon with Just a Knife

Step 1: *Choose & Prepare the Wood*

⟶ *Find a knotless branch or small log 25–30 centimetres long and at least 4 centimetres thick.*

⟶ *Baton the wood in half to create a flat working surface.*

Step 2: *Outline the Spoon Shape*

⟶ *Lightly sketch the spoon shape onto the wood.*

⟶ *The bowl should be oval, and the handle should be long enough for a comfortable grip.*

Tip: *If you don't have a pencil, score the outline with shallow knife cuts, or a piece of charcoal.*

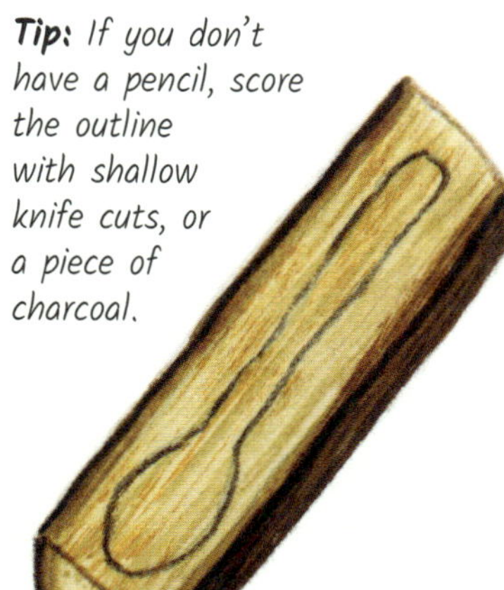

Step 3: *Shape the Outer Bowl & Handle*

⟶ *Gradually thin and shape the handle, ensuring it's sturdy but comfortable.*

⟶ *Carve around the bowl, rounding the edges.*

⟶ *We are just looking for the rough shape here, will refine later.*

Tip: *Avoid making the handle too thin – it could snap.*

Step 4: *Carve the Spoon's Bowl*

⟶ *Hold the wood securely and start hollowing out the bowl.*

⟶ *Use small, controlled cuts, working in a circular motion.*

Tip: *Green wood is softer and easier to carve than dry wood.*

Step 5: *Refine & Smooth the Spoon*

⟶ *Carefully shave off rough edges and refine the shape.*

⟶ *If available, use sand or a fine stone to smooth the surface.*

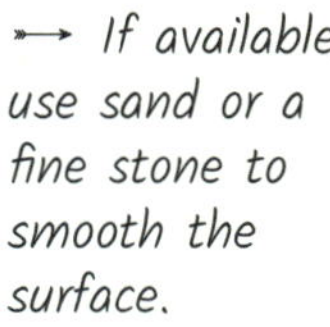

Step 6: *Dry & Harden the Spoon*

⟶ *Let the spoon dry naturally for a few days to prevent cracking.*

⟶ *Lightly harden it by a fire (don't burn it!).*

⟶ *If possible, oil it with animal fat, plant oil or beeswax to protect the wood.*

MAKE NATURAL CORDAGE

Physicists study string theory, but bushcrafters live it! Making cordage from natural fibres is one of the most useful – and satisfying – skills in the wild. With a little patience and the right material, you can twist plants into strong, handmade rope. The oldest known string was made by Neanderthals in France over 50,000 years ago. Proof that even during the Ice Age, survival starts with simple strands and skilled hands.

Where to Find Cordage Material

Nature is full of string – if you know where to look. Here are the best spots to find strong, flexible fibres in the wild:

Inner bark (basswood, cedar, willow, pine)

Strip the outer bark from dead branches to reach the tough, stringy layer beneath. That 50,000-year-old-string? It came from the inner bark of a conifer, likely pine.

Tree roots (spruce, pine, cedar)

Dig near young trees for pencil-thin roots. Great for lashing and strong cord.

Dry grasses (canary, bulrush, iris)

Look in meadows, marsh edges and ditches. Best when fully dried and crackly.

Stinging nettle & dogbane

Widespread in disturbed ground and at forest edges. Strip the outer stalks to reveal strong fibres.

Bonus: *Cooked nettle leaves are edible and packed with nutrients.*

Vines (grape, clematis, honeysuckle)

Woody vines grow along forest edges, up trees and over shrubs. Twist and test – some snap, others are perfect for light-duty lashing.

How to Prep Wild Fibres

Step 1: ***Collect.*** *Gather long fibres – inner bark, stalks or roots – at least 60–100 centimetres, if possible. The longer, the better.*

Step 2: ***Soak if Needed.*** *If the material feels stiff or brittle (like bark or roots), soak it in water until it's flexible. Some grasses are ready as is if fully dry.*

Step 4: ***Test for Twist.*** *Give it a try – twist a short piece. If it holds together without snapping or fraying, it's ready.*

Cordage Unlocks Survival

It's one of the few skills that ties almost everything else together – literally. Here's what cordage unlocks:

- *Tie together shelter frames*
- *Lash tools or tie equipment*
- *Make a bow drill for fire*
- *Weave nets or small-game traps*
- *Hang food off the ground*
- *Improvise sandals or snowshoes*
- *Create snares or fishing line*

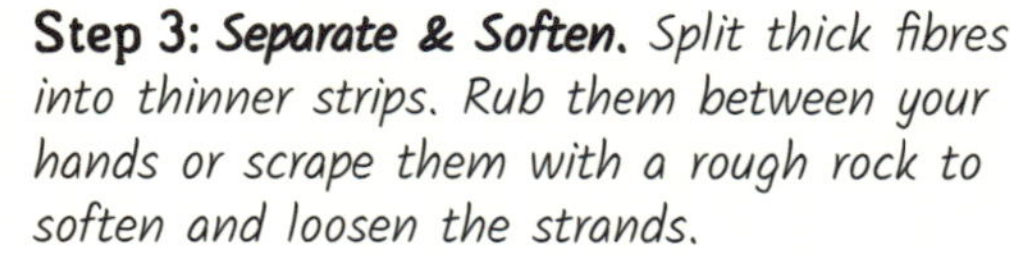

Step 3: ***Separate & Soften.*** *Split thick fibres into thinner strips. Rub them between your hands or scrape them with a rough rock to soften and loosen the strands.*

How to Prep Cordage

Step 1: ***Twist to Form the Eye.*** *Hold the fibre at its centre with one hand on each side, about 10 centimetres apart. Twist each side in opposite directions – right side clockwise, left side anticlockwise – until it kinks into a loop. That loop is your starting 'eye'.*

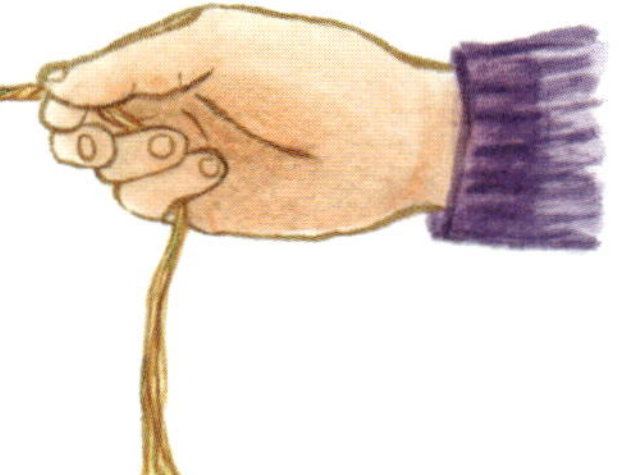

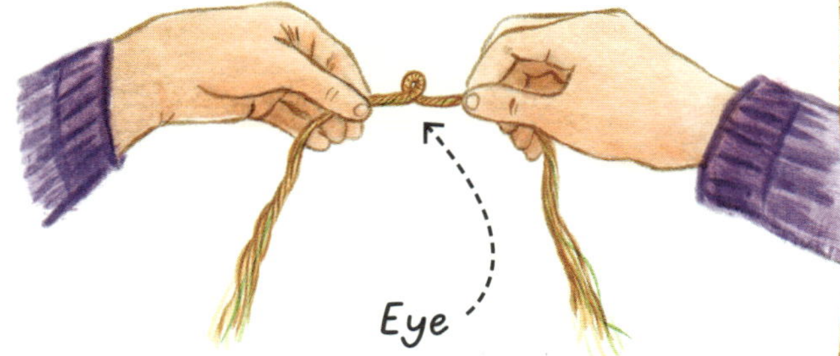

Step 2: ***Pinch & Anchor.*** *Hold the eye between your thumb and finger with one hand. You'll work the strands with your other hand from here.*

Step 3: ***Twist & Wrap.*** *Use your free hand to twist the bottom strand away from you (clockwise), then wrap it over the top strand. It now becomes the new top strand.*

Step 4: ***Repeat the Pattern.*** *Twist the new bottom strand away from you, wrap it over again.*

Twist away, cross over. Repeat. You'll see rope forming as you go.

Step 5: ***Add Fibres When Needed.*** *When a strand runs short, overlap a new piece and keep twisting. The tension locks it in.*

It gets easier fast – practise with some string at home and you'll have the rhythm in no time!

TIE KNOTS

Knots are some of the oldest technology on the planet. We pass them down because they work – strong, fast and easy to untie when you choose the right one. Learning a knot is like riding a bike: practise until it's muscle memory, and this skill will stay with you for life.

Parts of a Knot

Language is leverage – learn these before you start tying.

Working end
The end you're actively using to tie.

Standing part
The long length you're not tying with.

Bight
A U-shaped bend (no crossing).

Loop
A full circle where the rope crosses itself.

Tail
The free end left after the knot is set.

Most Useful Knots

You don't need a hundred knots. In the wild, these four will take you far.

Bowline (Fixed Loop)

Strong, non-slip loop. Easy to untie, even after a heavy load.

Step 1: ***Make the Hole***
Form a small loop in the standing part about 20–25 centimetres from the end, with the working end on top.

Tree

Rabbit hole

Rabbit

Step 2: ***Rabbit Up***
Feed the working end up through the loop.

Step 3: ***Around the Tree***
Go behind the standing part, then wrap to front.

Step 4: ***Back Down the Hole***
Feed it back down through the original loop.

Step 5: ***Tighten***
Hold the standing part and loop – pull the tail tight.

Clove Hitch (On a Bight)

Easily attach line to tent stakes, carabiners or sticks.

Step 1: *Make two identical loops, right next to each other, working end on top.*

Step 2: *Stack them on top of each other, right loop under left loop.*

Step 3: *Slip both loops over the stake or post.*

Step 4: *Pull both ends to tighten.*

Taut-Line Hitch

Adjusts tension without retying – perfect for ropes.

Step 1: *Wrap around the anchor and bring the working end back alongside the standing part.*

Step 2: *Make two wraps towards the anchor – around the standing part, inside the loop.*

Step 3: *Lock it with one wrap away from the anchor outside the loop. Pass the working end through the new loop.*

Step 4: *Dress the knot – tidy and snug – then pull tight. Slide to adjust; it should grip when loaded.*

Optional quick-release: *In Step 3, pass a bight through instead of the working end.*

Quick memory trick: *Two towards, one away; then it will stay.*

Slip-Loop Trucker's Hitch

Hardware-free pulley that cranks lines drum-tight.

Step 1: *Tie one end to a fixed point. Make a loop between the fixed point and anchor.*

Step 2: *Pull a bight through the loop and tighten to form a slip loop.*

Step 3: *Run the free end around the anchor and through the slip loop.*

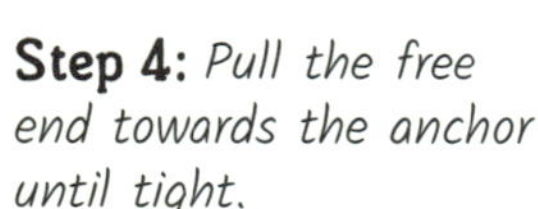

Step 4: *Pull the free end towards the anchor until tight.*

Step 5: *Tie off with two half hitches: wrap once, through the gap, snug and then repeat.*

Optional quick-release: *On the second half hitch, pull a bight through the gap.*

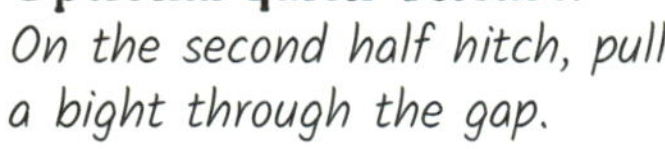

TRY LASHING

Lashing is the skill of binding two or more items together with rope. Wrapping an item with cord adds grip and brings the objects closer together. Tightening turns made around the wraps are called 'fraps' and cinch everything tight. This practice is centuries old but still incredibly useful today. Around camp, this means stronger shelter frames, pot hangers over the fire and simple camp furniture. Now let's build the most useful of them all – the tripod.

How to Lash a Tripod

Materials:

- Three straight poles (same length)
- 3–4.5 metres of cord

Step 1: ***Stage the Poles.*** Lay the three poles side by side. Mark the lashing spot 15–25 centimetres from the top.

Step 2: ***Start with a Clove Hitch.*** Tie a clove hitch on one outside pole at the mark. Snug it. (See page 34.)

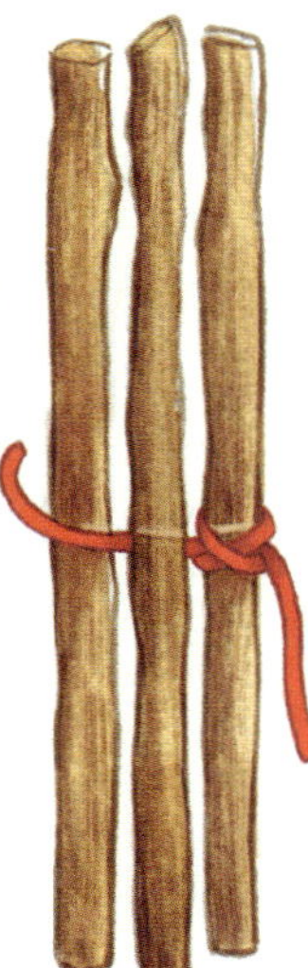

Step 3: ***Wrap the Bundle.*** Make five to seven racking turns: Weave the line in a figure eight between the poles, taking a snug turn around each outside pole on every pass. Keep cord neat and parallel – no crossing.

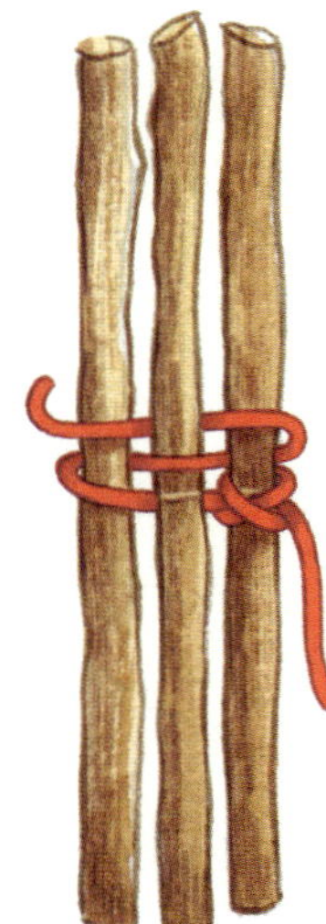

Step 4: ***Frap Between Poles 1 & 2.*** Pass the line through the gap between the first two poles. Take a tight turn straight around the wraps in that gap (one frap). Pull two to three fraps, snug and even, to cinch the lashing.

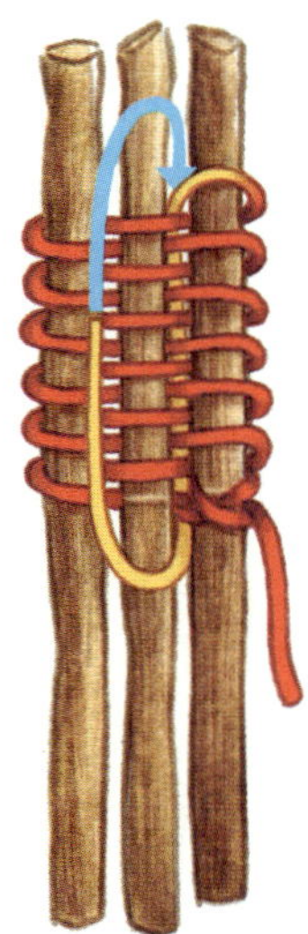

Step 5: ***Frap Between Poles 2 & 3.*** Repeat between poles 2 and 3. Two to three fraps.

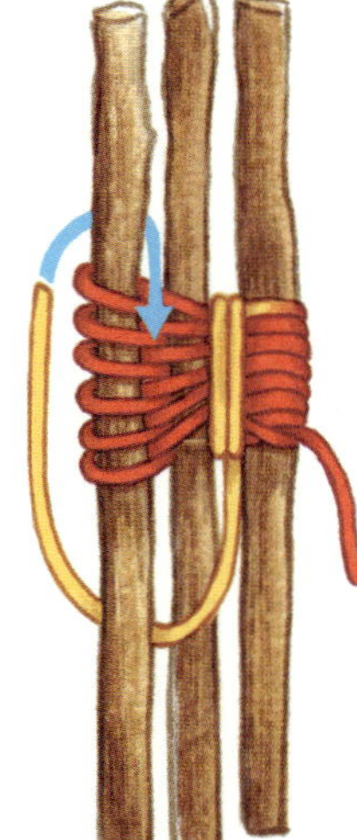

Tightness Tip:

Make wraps/racking turns firm and even. Keep fraps snug, but not too tight. If the legs won't spread, loosen the fraps a little and try again.

Step 6: ***Clove Hitch Finish.*** Tie off with a clove hitch on the outside pole. Trim or tuck in the tail.

Step 7: ***Stand & Spread.*** Stand the bundle upright and cross the two outside poles underneath the middle pole. This will tighten the lashing and hold the structure in place.

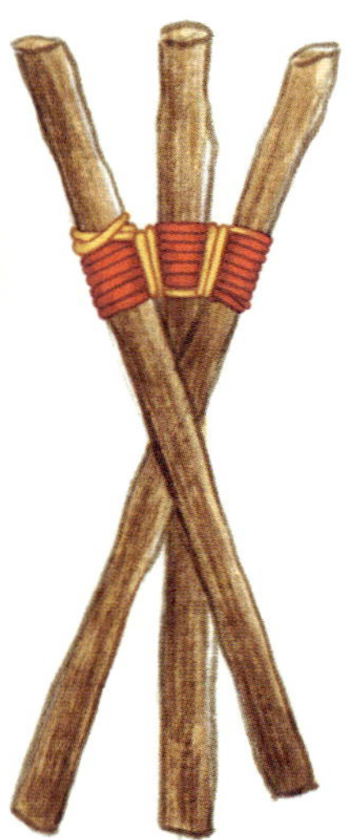

READ A RIVER

Rivers are the lifeblood of the countryside – winding through forests, carving valleys and nourishing everything in their path. Like nature's arteries, they carry life across the land, and learning to read them is a skill as old as civilisation itself. Ancient Egyptians built their world around the Nile, and many explorers followed rivers to food, shelter and adventure. A river always has a story to tell – you just have to learn how to read them.

The Quiet Teachings of a River

Navigation

A river is a reliable tool for cross-country travel – it always flows downhill, and it's easy to follow on a map. By matching its curves and direction, you can figure out where you are, and if you're lost, following it downstream can often lead to roads, camps or help.

Weather clues

Calm, clear water suggests stable conditions. If the water is turning muddy or rising quickly, be cautious – it could signal an approaching storm or even a flash flood upstream.

Best fishing spots

Focus on deep pools, bends and submerged trees where fish hide and rest. Look for areas with slower currents or where overhanging branches provide cover – those are prime places to cast your line!

The River Provides

Fresh water and fish are obvious, but check out all these other natural resources you can find in or near a river.

Clay & mud

Useful for building, cooking and creating tools (like simple pottery).

Reeds

Ideal for natural shelters, weaving baskets, flotation aids, or even primitive footwear.

Cordage

Plants like cattails and wild vines that can be braided or twisted into sturdy natural rope.

Edible plants

Watercress, wild mint, bulrushes, stinging nettles and other edible riverbank plants.

Driftwood & deadfall

Dry wood for fires, shelter frames or a walking stick.

Stones

Toolmaking materials for blades, grinding surfaces or fire-starting.

Insects & worms

Protein-rich survival food and bait for fishing.

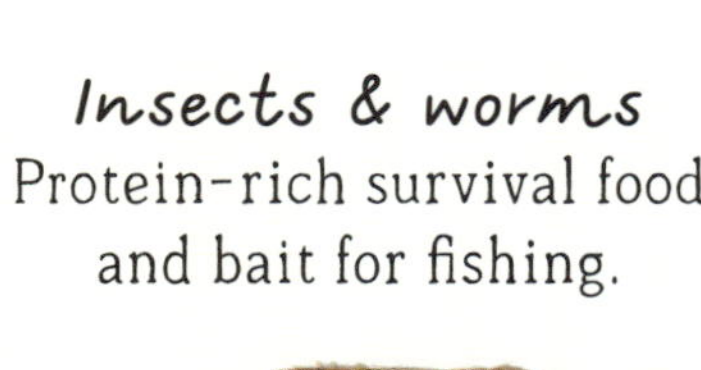

Animal tracks

Rivers attract wildlife, making it easier to hunt or observe animals from a distance.

Tip:

Do not eat anything in the wild unless you're certain what it is. Ask an adult for help.

A Step-by-Step Guide to Crossing a River Safely

This is one of the most vital skills you can learn in the wilderness. Always bring an adult, and keep this in mind: when in doubt – stay out!

Step 1: ***Scout the Spot.***
Look for a wide, shallow area with a slow current. Avoid deep, narrow or fast-moving spots.

Step 2: ***Keep Your Shoes On.***
Always cross with your shoes or boots on. Bare feet can slip or get cut on rocks. Wet shoes are better than hurt feet, or a fall in the water.

Step 3: ***Unbuckle Your Pack.***
Unclip your rucksack hip and sternum straps, so you can drop it quickly if you fall. It could save your life.

Step 4: ***Use a Stick or Pole.***
Find a sturdy stick taller than your waist. Use it like a third leg to feel the riverbed and keep balance.

Step 5: ***Face Upstream & Shuffle Sideways.***
Turn slightly towards the current and move sideways, one step at a time. Keep two points of contact – stick and foot – with each step.

Step 6: ***Take Your Time.***
Stay calm. Don't rush. Strong footing beats speed every time. If things feel uncertain, go back.

Safety Tip:

As the sun rises high into the sky, melting snow and ice can raise water levels fast – so morning is usually the safest time to cross.

MAKE A POCKET FISHING KIT

A pocket fishing kit might be small, but in the right hands, it's magic – turning a river into a source of food and adventure. Fishing teaches patience, sharpens survival skills and brings you closer to nature. Even in medieval Europe, people crafted simple travel fishing kits while on the move to catch perch and pike. And a fresh, fire-cooked trout might be the best meal on Earth.

Elements of a Pocket Fishing Kit

This kit should fit in a small pouch or resealable bag.

Line – A small spool of 6–10 pound test is ideal for small to medium-sized fish

Bobbers – Tiny floats to show when a fish bites

Hooks – A variety of sizes, from extra-small to medium

Lures or flies – A couple of simple lures or flies to attract fish

Sinkers – Small weights to help your bait sink

Bait – Dried or artificial, or go natural and use worms

Swivels – To keep your line from twisting

Rod – A collapsible rod or sturdy stick

Tip:

Check to see if you need a fishing license before heading out.

Tie a Fishing Hook

To do this, you'll need to master the clinch knot, which is easy, reliable, and perfect for keeping your swivel, lure or hook in place.

Step 1: *Thread your line through the eye of the hook.*

Step 2: *Take the working end and wrap it around the standing line five times.*

Step 3: *Pass the working end through the loop.*

Step 4: *Pull both ends to tighten.*

Step 5: *Cut off any excess.*

Step 6: *You're ready to fish!*

Wild Fishing Tips

Match the meal
Choose bait or lures that look like what fish are already eating – bugs, minnows or worms. Experiment until you find something that works.

Fish early or late
Dawn and dusk are when fish are most active – the light is low, bugs are out and the water feels safer to feed in.

Patience with a plan
If nothing's biting after a few tries, switch spots. Fishing takes patience – sometimes it's quiet for hours, then suddenly it's non-stop action!

Go with the flow
In rivers or streams, cast upstream and let your line drift naturally down. That's how real food moves.

Stay stealthy
Move slowly, stay low and keep your shadow off the water. Spook the fish, and they're gone.

Find the hiding spots
Cast near logs, boulders, deep pools or shady banks – that's where fish like to hang out.

A Step-by-Step Guide to Cooking Fish Over a Campfire

Roasting trout over a campfire by a mountain lake might be one of life's great pleasures. Here's how to do it.

Step 1: ***Clean Your Fish.*** *Open the fish by slicing the belly, from the tail to gills. Remove the guts and rinse with clean water.*

Step 2: ***Add Some Flavour.*** *If you packed salt, pepper or lemon, rub the inside of the fish with it.*

Step 3: ***Make a Cooking Stick.*** *Find a sturdy green stick (about as thick as your thumb). Sharpen one end and push it through the fish, through the mouth to the tail.*

Step 4: ***Prep Cooking Fire.*** *Let your campfire burn down until you've got glowing coals, not big flames. That's the best heat for cooking.*

Step 5: ***Cook Low and Slow.*** *Prop your skewer over the coals. Rotate it now and then. Don't rush. You're looking for flaky meat and crispy skin, 10–15 minutes depending on fish size.*

Step 6: ***Test for Doneness.*** *Poke the thickest part with your knife. If it flakes easily and isn't translucent, it's done.*

Step 7: ***Enjoy & Clean Up.*** *Cool for a few minutes, peel off the skin and enjoy! Just watch out for bones. Don't leave fish guts or bones around, as animals will find them. Burn scraps in the fire or pack them out.*

Common Freshwater Fish

These fish are very tasty and can be caught with a minimal kit.

GO FORAGING

Foraging is the art of finding wild food – plants, berries, mushrooms and more. Humans have gathered from the land for thousands of years, guided by need, curiosity and tradition. Even Ötzi the Iceman, a 5,000-year-old mummy found in the Alps, carried birch polypore mushrooms, likely for medicine or to fight off infection. It's time to tap back into that ancient knowledge and shop from nature's original grocery shop!

The Forager's Code

Be 100% sure

Some plants and fungi are poisonous. If you can't positively ID it, don't eat it. Ask an adult to help.

Skip roadsides

Roadside plants and fungi may absorb toxins from exhaust and run-off.

Harvest with care

Take a little, leave the rest so it can regrow and feed others.

Know the rules

Check local laws and get permission on private land.

Pack smart

Bring a basket, a knife, water and hiking essentials.

Easy Edibles: Berries, Greens & Herbs

The wild is full of edible plants and fungi – thousands, in fact. But here are a few of my all-time favourites to get you started!

Wood sorrel

Three heart-shaped leaves and a lemony snap. Not clover. A small, tasty trail nibble.

Blackberry

Thorny canes, white flowers and dark juicy berries. Ripe when they pull off easily.

Rose hip

The fruit of wild roses. Red-orange, oval and full of vitamin C. Best after the first frost.

Dandelion

Leaves, flowers and even roots are edible. Young leaves are best – mildly bitter.

Chickweed

Delicate green with tiny white star-shaped flowers. Mild flavour, like baby spinach.

Red clover

Pink-purple flower heads. Sweet and mild when young. Makes a great tea or salad topper.

Wild Strawberry

Tiny, fragrant and sweet. Look for three-toothed leaves and small red berries close to the ground.

Nettle

Serrated leaves with stinging hairs. Use gloves to pick, then cook or dry to remove the sting. Tastes like earthy spinach.

Mushroom Magic: Delectable Edibles

Survival food? Definitely. But wild mushrooms like morels can also be found on five-star menus! Here are some top picks:

Chanterelle
Golden or white, vase-shaped, with wavy edges and ridges instead of true gills. Fruity aroma, firm texture.

Morel
Hollow and cone-shaped with a honeycomb surface. Deeply prized and easy to spot with practice.

King bolete (porcini)
Thick stem, brown cap and spongelike pores underneath. Meaty and rich in flavour.

Hedgehog mushroom
Pale orange with soft spines (not gills) under the cap. Dense and nutty when cooked.

Oyster mushroom
Fan-shaped caps growing in layered clusters. Pale to grey with a savoury flavour.

Cauliflower mushroom
Looks like a yellow-beige sea sponge or brain coral. Crunchy when cooked, with a mild, nutty taste.

Fungus Facts

Mushrooms aren't plants.
They belong to their own kingdom: fungi.

Earth's largest life-form!
A honey fungus in Oregon, USA, spans 5.6 kilometres underground.

Some glow in the dark.
Bioluminescent fungi can light up forest floors at night.

Fungi eat plastic.
Certain mushrooms can break down synthetic waste.

They breathe like us.
Fungi take in oxygen and release carbon dioxide.

Warning:

Mushrooms can be seriously poisonous. Never rely solely on a book or app to identify them and always ask an adult who is an experienced forager to help you.

COOK OUTDOORS

Archaeologists found evidence of million-year-old hearths in Wonderwerk Cave, South Africa. Inside were layers of ash and charred animal bone – clear signs that early humans used fire to cook. Not much has changed. In the wild, life slows down, and food becomes the highlight. It's just a fact: from crispy trout to gooey s'mores – food tastes better when it's cooked outdoors.

Building a Cooking Fire

Cooking fires are different from warmth fires. Big flames can burn food fast. What you want is steady, even heat from a bed of glowing coals.

Try a keyhole fire – build your main fire to one side, and scrape hot coals into a flat 'cooking zone'. It gives you heat where you want it, and space to add fuel without kicking ash into your food.

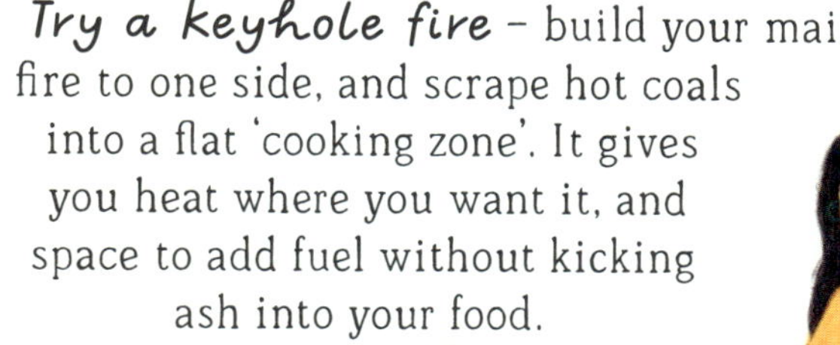

Build small – a compact fire is easier to control and better for cooking. Use a teepee or log cabin style to start, then feed it until you've got steady coals.

Think like an animal – bears can smell from over 30 kilometres away. In bear country, cook downwind and store food at least 90 metres from camp. Leave no crumb behind.

Use dry hardwood – avoid green wood, wet wood or softwoods like pine. They smoke a lot and don't burn hot for long.

Ways to Cook Over a Fire

Stick roasting – hot dogs, sausages, quick-cooking breads like bannock, marshmallows – if you can stab it, you can roast it. Use a green (live) stick so it won't burn through. Hold it low and slow over the coals.

Flat rock griddle – find a flat rock and set it near the fire to preheat, or prop it over the fire like a bridge. Cook directly on the surface – great for eggs, bacon or pancakes. Test it with a drop of water – it should sizzle.

One pot meals – Got a small pot? That opens the door to soups, pasta, stews, porridge – even hot drinks.

Rotating skewer – for longer cooking, like meat or veggies, carve a sturdy skewer and rest it across two Y-shaped sticks planted in the ground. Adjust the height to control the heat. It's a do-it-yourself rotisserie.

Cooking grate – rest it on rocks over your coals. Endless options – grilled cheese, kebabs, quesadillas. A small, foldable grate that packs down easily works best.

Tip:

Do as much prep as you can at home. Chop veggies, marinate meat, even pre-mix meals if it helps. It makes camp cooking easier – and clean-up way faster.

How to Make Banana Boats

This campfire dessert requires no dishes. Banana peels are naturally heat-resistant and rarely catch fire – making them the perfect cooking vessel. This is one of my all-time faves!

What you need:

- A ripe banana (not overripe)
- Knife
- Toppings: chocolate, mini marshmallows, crushed nuts, peanut butter, etc.
- A campfire with a bed of glowing coals

Step 1: ***Slice the Banana (Peel On).*** *Use a knife to slice the banana lengthwise, through the top of the peel and just into the fruit. Don't cut all the way through – make a little pocket.*

Step 2: ***Stuff It.*** *Gently open the peel and fill the banana with your favorite toppings. Pack it in! Chocolate, marshmallows, nut butter – whatever makes you smile.*

Step 3: ***Nestle It in the Coals.*** *Find a hot spot near the edge of the fire. Carefully set the banana directly on the coals, uncut peel-side down.*

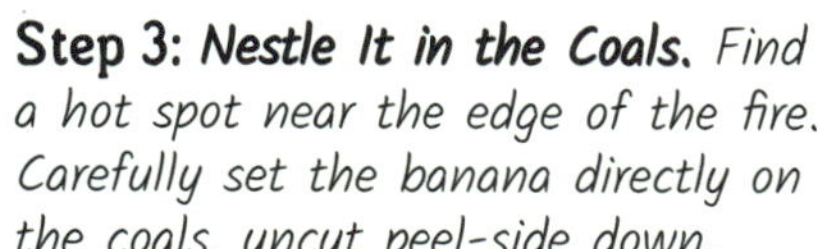

Step 4: ***Let It Cook (5–10 min).*** *Watch it closely. You'll see the peel blacken and toppings get melty – once the inside is gooey, it's ready.*

Step 5: ***Cool & Enjoy.*** *Let it cool for a minute. Peel back the skin and dig in with a spoon. Yum!*

IDENTIFY ANIMAL TRACKS AND SCAT

Animals are masters of hide and seek. They can slip through the woods without making a sound – but there are always signs of them to spot: a paw print in mud, fur on a branch or a pile of scat. It's nature's version of storytelling. For thousands of years, people have followed these clues – not just to survive, but to understand the world around them. When you learn to read the land this way, every walk becomes more of an adventure, bringing you closer to the wild lives just out of sight.

Scat Happens: Reading Poo Like a Pro

Scat is one of the best clues you can find in nature. Every animal leaves a different signature behind – like a poo fingerprint (a pooprint, if you will). Some are tidy little pellets, others are twisty, lumpy or full of fur, seeds or even bones. By paying attention to shape, size, content and location, you can figure out what animal was there, what it was eating and even how recently it passed through. Just remember – use your eyes, not your fingers!

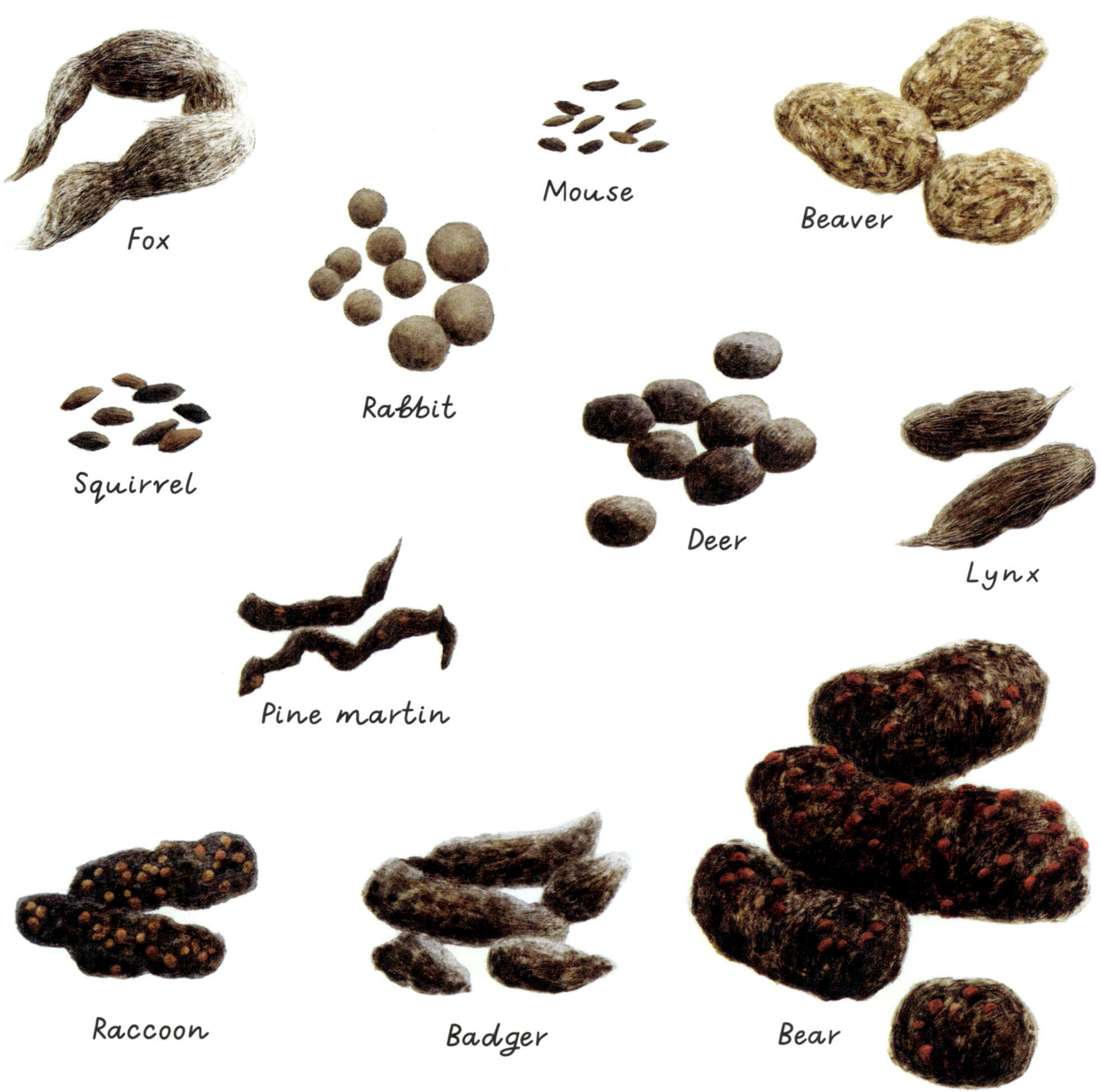

Reading Animal Tracks Like a Forest Detective

Just like scat, animal tracks are nature's way of saying, "I was here, but you just missed me!" Each print can reveal so much: who passed through, how fast they were moving and what direction they were headed. Some tracks are crisp and clear, like a stamp, while others are smudgy puzzles that test your detective skills!

Animal tracks can look very different, but animals in the same group often leave similar kinds of prints. Here's what to look for:

Birds
Most birds leave a 'peace sign' shape with three front toes and one back toe.
Pheasant
Hopping birds leave pairs of tracks. Walking birds leave alternating ones.
Blackbird
Reptiles and amphibians, like lizards and snakes
Lizards may show widespread toes and sometimes tail drag marks.
Lizard
Snakes don't have feet, but they may leave wavy lines in soft dirt or sand.
Snake
Small mammals, like rabbits and squirrels
Back feet are bigger, and usually appear in front of the grouping.
Pine martin
Rabbit
Mouse
Squirrel
Their tracks usually show a hopping or bounding pattern.

PREDICT THE WEATHER

Long before weather apps or radar maps, people read the sky like a book. A shift in the wind, a ring around the moon or the way birds flew could mean the difference between safety and disaster. Some of the oldest written forecasts come from Babylonians, who studied clouds to predict storms over two thousand years ago. Learning to read the sky keeps that ancient wisdom alive.

Reading Nature's Clues

Look, listen, feel – nature always drops hints if you know how to spot them.

Clouds

High and wispy = fair skies.

Low, thick or growing tall = rain or storms.

Fast-changing clouds mean a shift is coming.

Wind

A sudden change in wind direction or speed often means a front is moving in – warm winds before, cool winds after.

Body cues (pressure changes)

A drop in air pressure can cause headaches, joint pain or that heavy, 'storm's coming' feeling. Animals sense it too.

Sun & moon halos

A glowing ring around the sun or moon means high moisture – often a sign of rain within 24 hours.

Smell

Scents travel better in humid air. Stronger earthy or plant smells = higher moisture = possible rain.

Animal behaviour

Birds change flight patterns. Insects vanish. Many animals sense weather shifts before we do.

Clouds Tell a Story

Every change in weather starts with a change in the clouds. Learn to read them, and you'll stay one step ahead.

Cirrus

Thin and wispy, like brushstrokes in the sky. Fair weather now, but change may be coming.

Altostratus

Grey or blue-grey sheets that blanket the sky. The sun may shine through faintly, but light rain is likely on the way.

Stratus

Flat and grey, like a foggy blanket. Often brings drizzle or light rain.

Cumulonimbus

Massive towers reaching through all layers are thunderstorm clouds, bringing lightning, heavy rain and maybe hail.

Cumulus

Big, puffy and bright – classic fair-weather clouds. But if they grow tall, a storm could follow.

Signs a Storm Is Coming

The 'calm before the storm' isn't just a saying – it's a signal.

Sudden stillness

Wind dies down before a storm, especially thunderstorms. The calm can feel eerie.

Humid, heavy air

When moisture builds and the air feels thick, it often means rain is on the way.

Drop in temperature

A sudden chill, especially after warm wind, can signal a cold front pushing in.

Growing dark clouds

If clouds are rising fast and turning grey or black, especially from the west – get ready.

Flashes of distant lightning

Even without thunder, lightning in the distance means a storm could be heading your way.

Nature gets quiet – except the frogs

Birds go silent. Insects hush. But frogs, toads and crickets often get louder before a storm, especially when the air turns damp.

I've spent hours at camp with storms rolling overhead – reading, resting and listening to the rain. I genuinely love those moments. But being settled in before the sky breaks? That's everything.

USE A COMPASS

Imagine hiking in a forest in the pouring rain. You're miles from any trail and out of nowhere your GPS quits working. If you have a compass and know how to use it, you can navigate back home safely. In a world ruled by screens, using a compass has become a forgotten skill. Remember – tech fails and signals vanish. If you're exploring on foot, this is an essential skill to master.

Cardinal Directions are the four main directions on a compass. Think of your compass like a clock:

North → 12 o'clock
East → 3 o'clock
South → 6 o'clock
West → 9 o'clock

An easy way to remember? 'Never Eat Shredded Wheat'.

Meet Your Compass

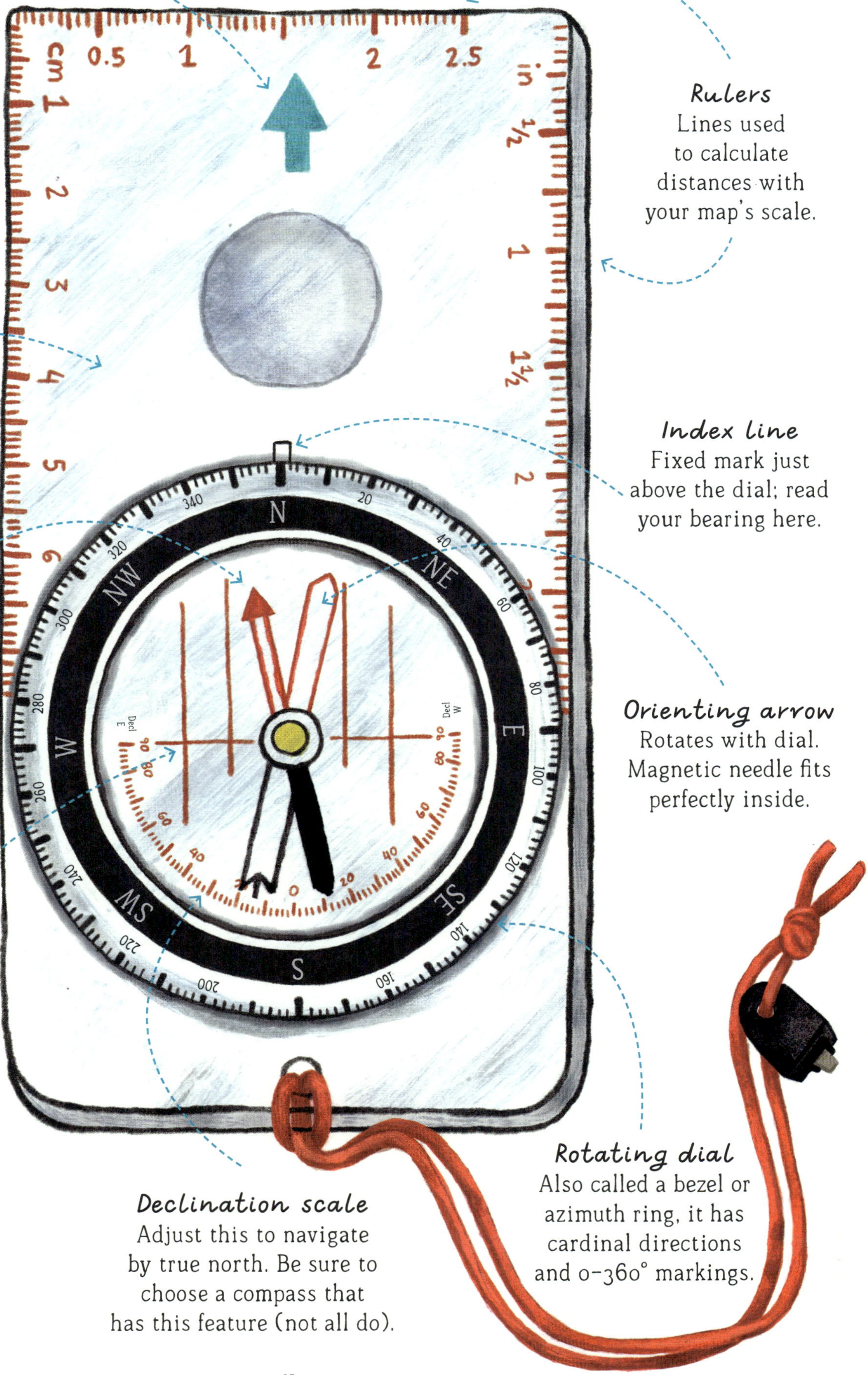

Direction-of travel arrow
Small triangle at the front of baseplate. Points in the direction you will be travelling.

Rulers
Lines used to calculate distances with your map's scale.

Baseplate
Flat body of the compass. It's clear, so you can see the map through it.

Index line
Fixed mark just above the dial; read your bearing here.

Magnetised needle
Always points to magnetic north. It's usually red or white.

Orienting arrow
Rotates with dial. Magnetic needle fits perfectly inside.

Orienting lines
Parallel lines inside the dial; line them up with the map's north-south grid.

Declination scale
Adjust this to navigate by true north. Be sure to choose a compass that has this feature (not all do).

Rotating dial
Also called a bezel or azimuth ring, it has cardinal directions and 0–360° markings.

Understanding Declination

Before you use a compass, you need to set the declination. It helps to know these terms first:

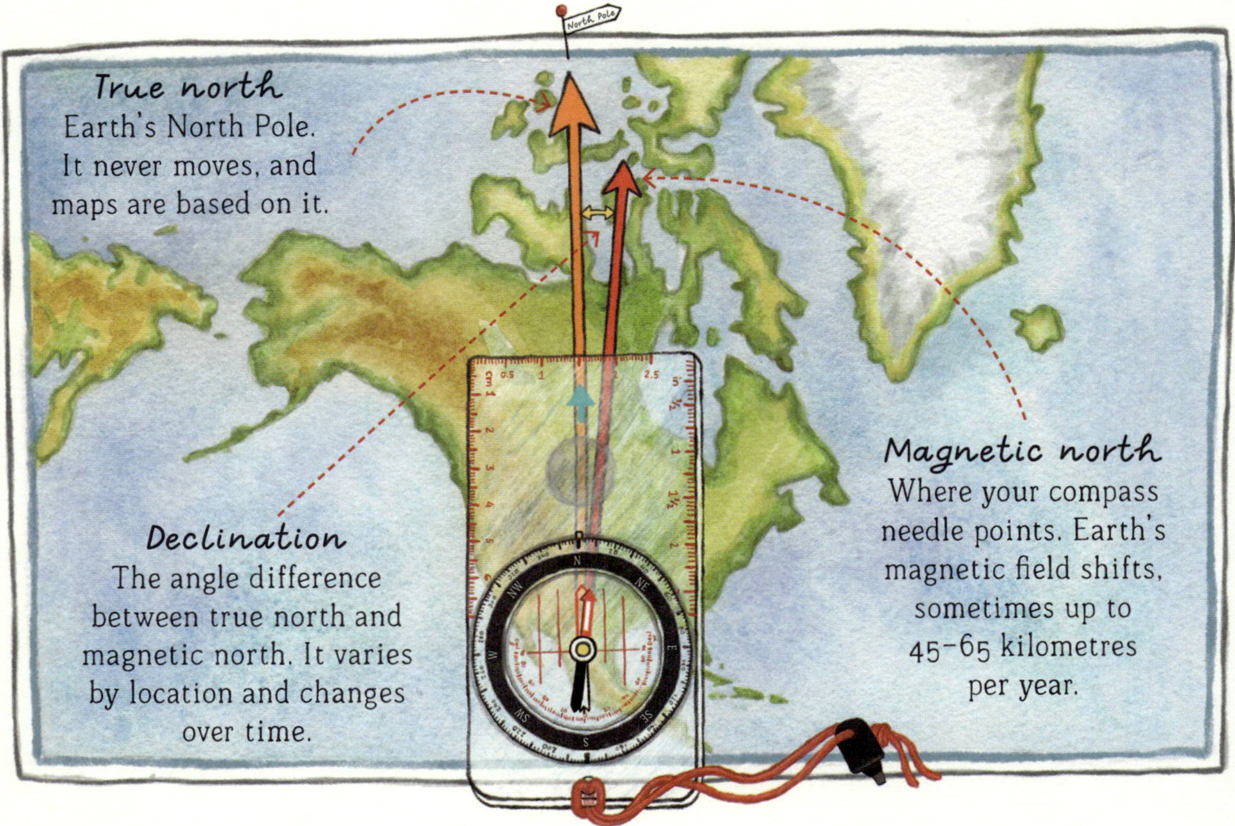

Set Declination on Compass

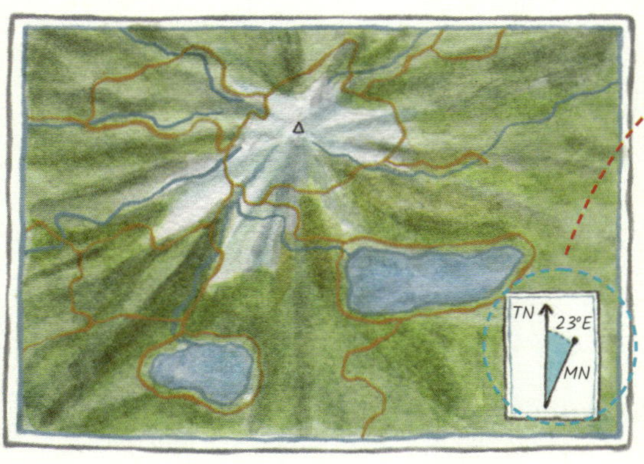

Step 1: *Find the declination value for your area. It's often printed on maps but may be outdated. For the latest value, use the free NOAA online calculator.*

Step 2: *Set that value on your compass. The method varies by brand, so check your compass's instructions.*

Tip:

Re-check your declination once a year – or any time you explore a new region where magnetic north differs significantly.

Orienting Your Map

Orienting your map means turning it until it precisely matches the land around you. Once it's aligned, the hills, valleys, lakes and mountains on paper line up with what you see, helping you understand exactly where you are.

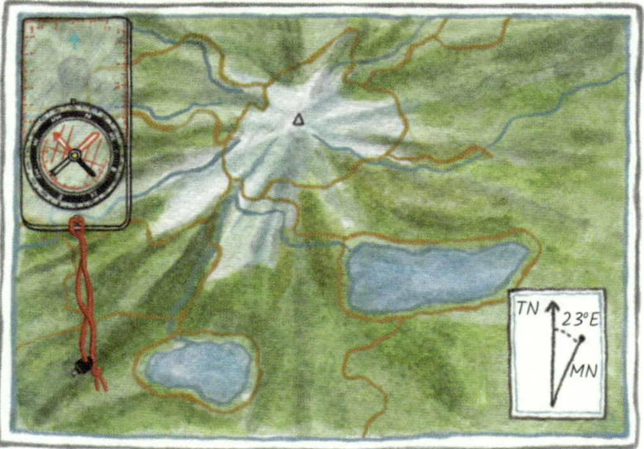

Step 1: ***Place Your Compass.*** *Set compass on map with the direction-of-travel arrow pointing towards the top (true north). Slide it so one straight edge lines up with the side of the map.*

Step 2: ***Set the Dial.*** *Rotate the dial until 'N' lines up with the direction-of-travel arrow.*

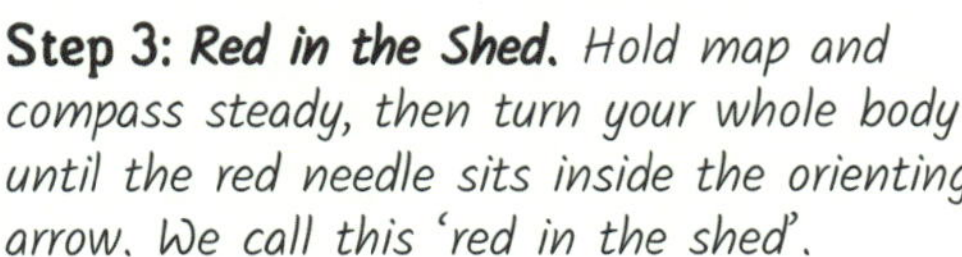

Step 3: ***Red in the Shed.*** *Hold map and compass steady, then turn your whole body until the red needle sits inside the orienting arrow. We call this 'red in the shed'.*

Step 4: ***Confirm Orientation.*** *Your map now matches the land around you. Use it to spot landmarks and check it often as you hike – staying found is a lot easier than getting un-lost later.*

Travel by Bearing from Map

A 'bearing' is just a precise way to describe direction. Instead of saying 'go northwest', you'd say 'follow a bearing of 315°'.

Step 1: ***Find Your Route.*** *On your map, find where you are and where you want to go.*

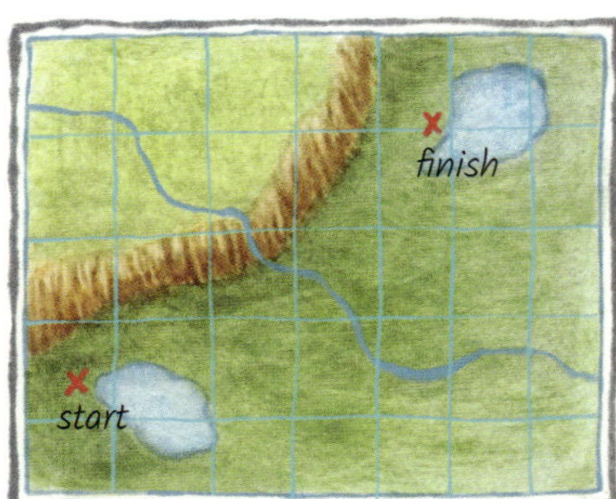

Step 2: ***Align Compass on Map.*** *Place the long edge of the compass from your location to destination. The direction-of-travel arrow should point towards your destination.*

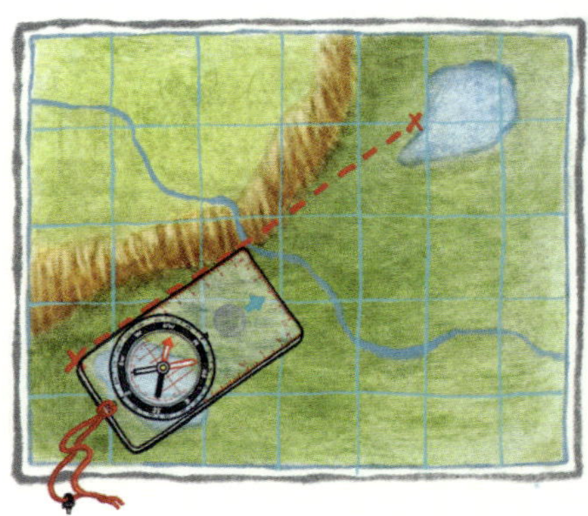

Step 3: ***Set the Bearing.*** *Rotate the dial until the orienting lines are parallel with the map's north–south grid lines. The orienting arrow points to the top of the map. The number below the index line is your bearing.*

Step 4: ***Lift & Find Red in the Shed.*** *Pick up the compass and hold it level in front of you. Turn your body until the magnetic needle sits inside the orienting arrow (red in the shed).*

Step 5: ***Travel on the Bearing.*** *Look ahead and pick a landmark in line with your direction-of-travel arrow. Keep red in the shed, and walk to that point. Repeat with new landmarks as you go. This is faster and easier than staring at the compass nonstop.*

Important: *Using your compass? Keep it clear of phones, electronics and metal objects. Magnetic fields can throw off your bearing.*

Make a Floating Needle Compass

You can do this for fun at home – or it could save you in an emergency.

Materials:

- Sewing needle or pin
- Magnet (fridge magnet works)
- Flat leaf or piece of cork
- Bowl or puddle of still water

Step 1: ***Magnetise the Needle.*** *Hold the needle and stroke the magnet one way only along its length about 50 times.*

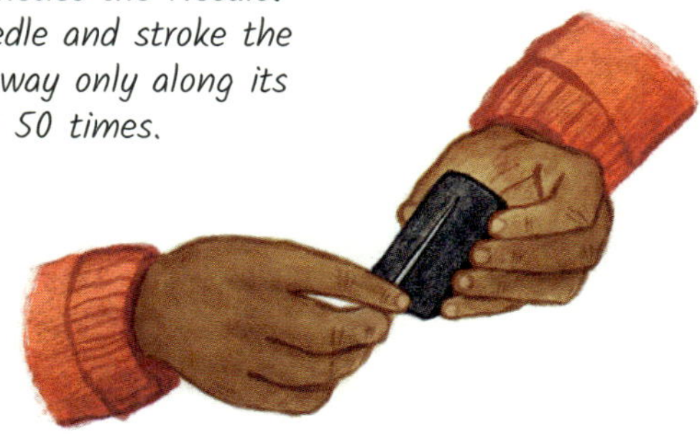

Step 2: ***Prepare the Float.*** *Use a flat leaf, thin cork slice or other light material that will hold the needle and float freely.*

Step 3: ***Mount the Needle.*** *Lay the needle gently across the leaf or push it through the cork lengthwise so it stays balanced.*

Step 4: ***Float It.*** *Set the leaf or cork in still water. Avoid moving water or windy spots.*

Step 5: ***Let It Settle.*** *The needle will slowly turn and point north–south. To find which end is north, remember: the sun rises in the east and sets in the west, and the four cardinal directions line up like a clock.*

No Magnet? *Rub the needle in one direction 50–100 times against your hair or wool clothing. The friction creates static electricity, temporarily magnetising the needle. It's weaker than using a real magnet, but works in an emergency.*

TELL THE TIME WITHOUT A CLOCK

Long before clocks existed, people used nature to tell the time, relying on the sun, moon and stars to track the hours. Polynesian navigators mastered this skill, using the night sky to cross vast oceans with incredible accuracy. It's a lost art in today's digital world, but mastering these time-telling tricks makes you feel like an explorer of the past, tuned into Earth's rhythms.

Return Before Dark

Tick-tock, nature talks. If you're out hiking or camping, keep your senses sharp, and pay attention to the sounds, sights and smells around you. Picking up on these clues will help you tell when sunset's coming – so you can make it back before dark!

Stretchy shadows – longer shadows mean the sun's getting lower. This is often a first signal that it's time to think about heading back.

Buzzing bugs – hear that hum? Mosquitoes and other bugs get busier as the day ends. Especially the last hour before sunset.

Trail traffic – noticing more hikers heading the other way? Well, most hikers are trying to make it back before dark too!

Golden hour glow – when everything looks golden and the light feels warm and soft – that's the golden hour. It happens the hour before sunset (and after sunrise). Everything can look more beautiful in this light, and it's a wonderful time to take pictures.

Smell the air – some scents get stronger in the evening. Plants release oils, damp earth smells more intense and wood smoke travels farther.

Active wildlife – many animals (like deer, rabbits and foxes) become more active in the hour before sunset.

Tip:

Be sure to give yourself extra time to get back. Also, always have a headlamp with extra batteries in your pack, just in case. Make that an essential if you're travelling on foot.

How Long Until Sunset?

You can estimate the time until sunset using just your hands. This technique works best in open areas with a clear view of the sun. It's surprisingly accurate, and a personal favourite of mine. Here's how to do it:

Step 1: ***Find the Sun & Horizon***

⟶ *Face the sun and hold your hand out at arm's length with your palm facing you.*

Step 2: ***Stack Your Fingers***

⟶ *Align the bottom of your pinkie finger with the horizon. Stack one hand on top of the other, until you reach the sun. Don't use your thumbs here.*

Step 3: ***Estimate Sunset***

⟶ *Add up hands and remaining fingers to get your estimate. Each finger represents about 15 minutes until sunset. A full hand (four fingers) equals one hour.*

3 hours and 45 minutes until sunset

2 hours until sunset

Remember: This skill also works with moonsets under the night sky!

Telling Time with the Moon

With a little practice, the moon becomes your cosmic clock! Here's how to use the moon's phases to estimate time.

New moon
Not visible.

Waxing crescent
Rises before noon, sets before midnight.

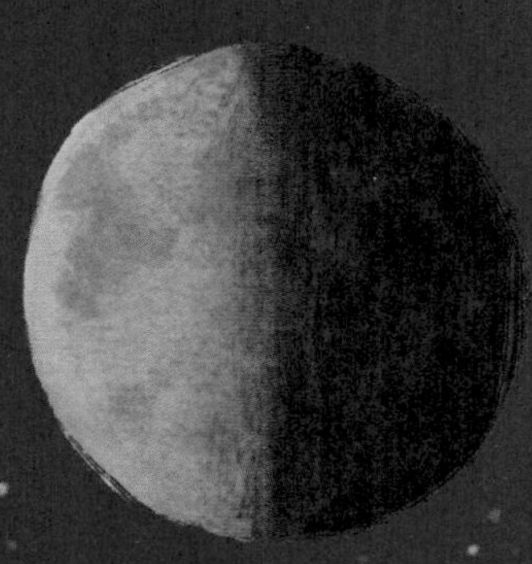

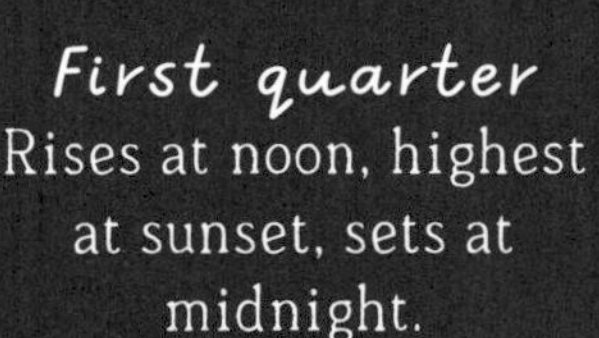

First quarter
Rises at noon, highest at sunset, sets at midnight.

Waxing gibbous
Rises after noon, sets after midnight.

Full moon
Rises at sunset, highest at midnight, sets at sunrise.

Waning gibbous
Rises after sunset, sets before noon.

Last quarter
Rises at midnight, highest at dawn, sets at noon.

Waning crescent
Rises before sunrise, sets before sunset.

A full moon is the easiest phase for estimating time, while a new moon leaves you in the dark – so always have a plan B!

STARGAZE AND FIND CONSTELLATIONS

Looking up at the night sky is like opening a window into the past. Explorers once sailed by starlight, and the ancients shaped entire monuments to match the heavens. The Egyptian pyramids of Giza still reflect the pattern of the constellation Orion – proof the sky once shaped Earth. It's not just a sky full of stars – it's the oldest classroom in the universe.

How the Night Sky Moves

That changing sky is proof you're rotating through space on a big blue ball. Learn the stars' patterns, and the sky becomes a giant rotating map.

Watch the stars move through the night – the stars appear to drift from east to west each night, because Earth is spinning at about 1,600 kilometres per hour!

See the sky change with the seasons – some constellations are easiest to see at certain times of the year, like Orion in winter.

Stargazing Tips:

- Pick a clear, dark night – new moon is best.
- Get away from city lights – light pollution hides the stars.
- Let your eyes adjust – give it 15–20 minutes.
- Bring a blanket – it's better when comfy.
- Use red light – it protects your night vision.

The Zodiac: 12 Star Signs in the Sky

Your zodiac sign is the constellation hidden behind the sun on your birthday – so you won't see it in the night sky until about six months later.

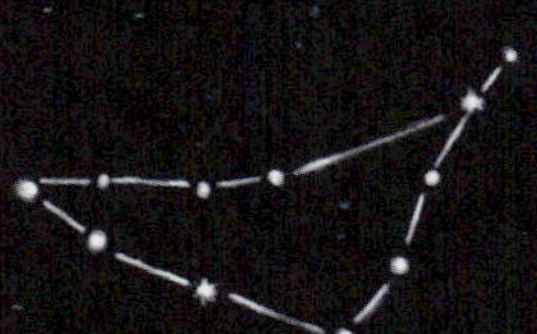

Capricorn
Goat
22 December–
19 January

Aquarius
Water bearer
20 January–
18 February

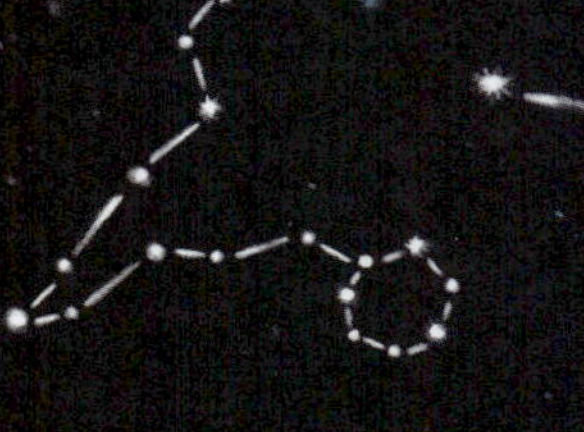

Pisces
Fish
19 February–
20 March

Aries
Ram
21 March–
19 April

Taurus
Bull
20 April–
20 May

Gemini
Twins
21 May–
20 June

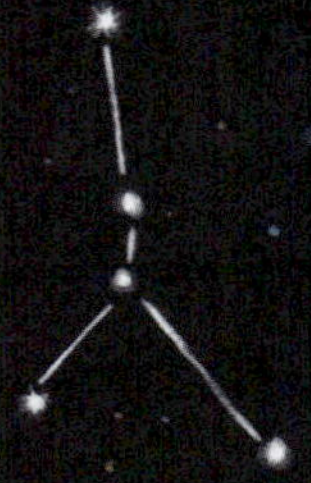

Cancer
Crab
21 June–
22 July

Leo
Lion
23 July–
22 August

Virgo
Maiden
23 August–
22 September

Libra
Scales
23 September–
22 October

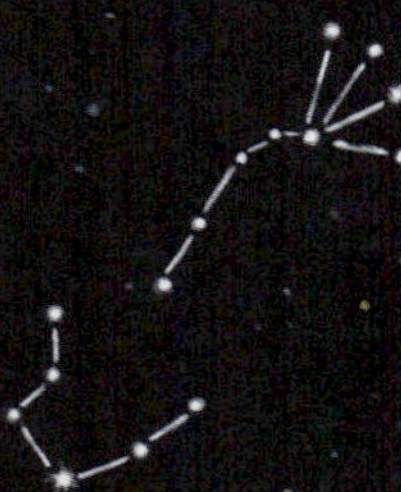

Scorpio
Scorpion
23 October–
21 November

Sagittarius
Archer
22 November–
21 December

How to Find the North Star

When it comes to finding your way in the Northern Hemisphere, no star is more valuable than Polaris. It's the only star that stays fixed in the sky, always marking true north. That's why it's also called the North Star.

Step 1: ***Find the Big Dipper.*** *It's one of the easiest star patterns to spot. Look for a group of seven bright stars shaped like a ladle or spoon.*

Step 2: ***Use the Pointer Stars.*** *Locate the two stars on the edge of the bowl opposite the 'handle'. These are called the pointer stars.*

Step 3: ***Draw a Line.*** *Imagine a straight line going up from the pointer stars, about five times the distance between them.*

Step 4: ***Spot the North Star.*** *That line leads to a single bright star: Polaris, the North Star!*

Step 5: ***Face it to Find Direction.*** *Once you've found Polaris, you're facing true north – with east to your right, west to your left and south behind you.*

WHAT TO DO IF YOU GET LOST

Getting lost in the wild can feel scary! Maybe you stepped off trail to go to the loo or check something out – and now the path is gone. With the right mindset and a few simple steps, you can stay safe, think clearly and find your way out or make it easier for help to find you. Even the best explorers go off track occasionally. Here's how to handle it.

S.T.O.P. + Backtrack Guide

If you ever feel a little lost out there, don't panic.
Remember S.T.O.P.:

S – Stop

Freeze. Don't run or wander. Sit down, breathe and calm your mind.

T – Think

Where were you last sure of the trail? What direction were you heading? Did you cross water or see anything unusual?

O – Observe

Look and listen. Can you hear water? See a marker? Notice the sun's direction or how much daylight is left? Check your map, compass or GPS.

P – Plan

Now decide what to do – stay put and shelter, or try to find your way back.

Stay Put or Backtrack?

Stay Put and Wait for Help If:

- You're unsure which way you came from.
- You're hurt, tired or it's late.
- The terrain is tricky or unsafe.
- Someone knows your route and will likely search for you.

Backtrack Only If:

- You clearly recognise a recent landmark or trail.
- You haven't gone far since last known location.
- You're calm, alert and it's safe to move.
- You use a spider search method.

The Spider Search: A Safe Way to Look Around

This method helps you explore safely without getting more lost.

Step 1: ***Mark Your Starting Point.*** *Pick a spot you can see from all sides. Stick a branch upright, tie something bright to it or stack rocks. This is home base.*

Step 2: ***Walk Straight in One Direction.*** *Pick a direction and walk slowly in a straight line. Look for foot prints, broken branches or anything familiar.*

Step 3: ***Drop Markers as You Go.*** *Every 20–30 steps, leave something behind – a stick in the ground, rock stack or paracord tied to a low branch. ALWAYS keep the last one in sight before placing the next.*

Step 4: ***Turn Back if You're Unsure.*** *If nothing looks familiar after a few markers, stop. Follow your trail back to home base.*

Step 5: ***Try a New Direction.*** *From home base, pick a new direction and repeat. If no luck after trying all directions, return to the first spoke and go farther.*

Essential Safety Tips

Tell someone your plans – before every trip, share your route and return time so someone can alert search and rescue if needed.

Always carry the essentials – be ready for an unexpected night out. Bring key items such as food, water, protective gear, matches and a torch or headlamp.

Stay near water if you stay put – shelter near water if possible. You can survive weeks without food – but only about three days without water.

Practise navigation often – stay sharp with your map, compass or GPS. The goal? Being able to navigate back easily if you take a wrong turn.

How to Signal for Help

- Move to a clearing for visibility from the air.
- Lay out bright equipment or clothing.
- Make a large X or an arrow using rocks, logs or cleared dirt.
- Blow a whistle (three blasts) or signal with a mirror or light.
- If it's safe, light a smoky fire by day or a bright fire at night.

APPLY FIRST AID

Out here, help isn't minutes away – it could be miles. Knowing basic first aid helps you stay calm, think clearly and take care of injuries when it counts. Even NASA has trained its astronauts to treat wounds and handle emergencies in the wild, just in case they landed off course after re-entry. Being prepared isn't just smart – it's essential.

Stay Calm, Act Smart

Your brain is your best first aid tool. When something goes wrong, don't panic. Slow down. Breathe. Staying calm helps you think clearly and act fast.

Pause and assess

Check the situation. Is anyone in danger? Are you safe where you are? Think before you move.

Stop bleeding first

Apply pressure with gauze or cloth. Elevate if possible. Bleeding control is step one.

Protect the wound

Clean it, cover it and keep it as dry and dirt-free as possible.

Support the injury

Sprains or breaks? Immobilize with a wrap or makeshift splint. Help the body rest.

Keep warm and watch for shock

If someone is pale, shaky or confused, lie them down, elevate their legs and keep them warm.

Too injured to hike out?

Stay put, stay safe and call for help. No working phone? Use your signalling skills – check the What to Do If You Get Lost section for how to get noticed.

Don't let this section scare you: I feel safer deep in the wild than I do on the drive there. After hundreds of nights in the wild, I've never had a serious injury.

What to Pack in a First Aid Kit
You can build your own or buy a premade one – just make sure it has what you need.
Gauze swabs & medical tape
Antiseptic wipes & ointment
Adhesive bandages (all sizes)
Tweezers & small scissors (multi-tool works)
Elastic bandage
Safety pins
Personal medications
Anti-itch cream or antihistamine
Pain relievers (like ibuprofen)
Field Favourite: First Aid Balm
A small tin of herbal first aid balm can be used on cuts, scrapes, sunburns, bug bites, chafing and even dry skin. It's a lightweight, all-purpose lifesaver that's a valuable addition to your kit.

Common Outdoor Injuries (and What to Do)

Cut or scrape

Clean it with water. Use gauze or a clean cloth to stop bleeding. Cover with a bandage to keep dirt out.

Blister

Don't pop it unless it's painful. Cover with a bandage or blister plaster to prevent rubbing.

Sprain or strain

Rest it. Wrap with a bandage or cloth for support. Elevate if you can, and cool it down with water or a wet cloth.

Insect bite or sting

Remove the sting if it's there. Wash the area and apply first aid balm. If swelling grows fast, seek help. Allergic to stings? Carry an EpiPen and know how to use it – it can save your life.

Burn (fire or sun)

Cool the area with clean water. Gently clean if needed. Cover loosely with gauze or cloth. For sunburn, a first aid balm speeds up healing.

Tick

Use tweezers to grasp the tick as close to the skin as possible. Pull straight out – slow and steady (no twisting). Clean the spot and keep an eye on it.

Minor allergic reaction

Itchy or red? An antihistamine can help. Watch for serious signs like swelling or trouble breathing.

WHAT TO DO IN A LIGHTNING STORM

In medieval times, people rang church bells during thunderstorms to scare off lightning and evil spirits. Today, we have a better understanding of lightning and how to protect ourselves. Respect the storm, know what to do and you can stay safe when the sky turns electric.

A Step-by-Step Guide to Lightning Storm Safety

Step 1: ***Act Fast.*** *If you hear thunder, get to lower ground immediately.*

Step 4: ***Avoid Metal Objects and Water.*** *Electricity travels easily through metal and water. Drop trekking poles and fishing rods, and stay clear of fences, poles and shorelines – 30 metres away if possible.*

Step 2: ***Get Off High Ground.*** *Lightning is attracted to high points – descend from hills, mountain peaks or ridges. Avoid tall lone trees.*

Step 5: ***Assume the Lightning Position.*** *Crouch low on the balls of your feet, heels touching, head tucked, hands over ears. Don't lie flat. If you have a foam pad, place it under your feet.*

Step 3: ***Seek Shelter and Spread Out.*** *Shelter in a stand of small trees or a dry ditch. Space out at least 6 metres from others. This reduces the chance of multiple injuries from one strike.*

Step 6: ***Wait It Out.*** *Stay put for at least 30 minutes after the last thunderclap. Lightning can strike long after the main storm passes.*

Tip:

Being in a car is one of the safest places to be in a lightning storm. (It works like a Faraday cage, blocking electromagnetic fields.) Great to know, in case you're car camping.

PLAY WILDERNESS GAMES

Before the invention of playgrounds or board games, people played in the dirt, the woods and the wild. Games taught skills, built teamwork and passed time around the fire. In some Inuit communities, listening and stalking games trained kids to move quietly and read wind, ice and distance – play that doubled as survival practice. Playing outside is nothing new, it's how we've always learned, laughed and connected.

Learn Skills, Have Fun

The best way to learn is through play!

Locate your spot (map race)

Taking a break? Pull out the map. The first person to pinpoint your location wins.

Stick toss (accuracy)

Stand behind a line. Aim for a target on the ground. Whoever's stick comes closest wins. This game builds hand-eye coordination, distance judgment and control.

Fastest knot tie

Everyone grabs a length of paracord. On 'go', tie a bowline knot. Whoever finishes first wins. Level up to clove hitch, taut-line or trucker's hitch.

Tallest rock stack

See how many rocks you can balance. Dismantle your stack completely before you leave, so the place looks natural for the next person.

One-word story

Sit in a circle, and ask each person to add one word to build a silly story. Keep it moving fast. It's the perfect fireside game.

Nature Connection Games

These help you listen better, notice more and feel like you're part of the place – not just a visitor.

Quiet game

If you talk, you're out. Scan the trees, rocks, water or moss. Try to spot ten things you hadn't noticed before.

Field sketch

Grab a notepad and pencil. Sit and draw a plant or scene. Who knows, this might be your gateway into becoming an artist!

Nature scavenger hunt

Flip through a local field guide. Pick something and try to find it. It's a great way to learn about the local trees, plants, berries and fungi.

Pattern spy

Spot natural patterns: spirals, symmetry, rings, hexagons, shingles.

Tip:

Competitive games are great when everyone's on the same level. If not, switch to coach mode – teaching or learning can be even more fun.

Make a Grass Whistle

Step 1: *Pick a wide, flat, fresh stalk of grass.*

Step 2: *Place grass flat between thumbs, ends sticking out. Make sure it's taut.*

Step 3: *Lightly seal the gap with your lips and blow like a whistle. You should hear a shrieking, whistling sound.*

Step 4: *Tighten/loosen thumbs, change angle/strength of blow for pitch. Can get wildly loud if done just right.*

Play a Song:

Copy the wind, the birds – then make your own tune.

THE SEVEN PRINCIPLES OF LEAVE NO TRACE

Leave No Trace (LNT) helps protect land, water and wildlife – keeping these places wild for the next hiker. They're science-based and field-tested, yet they echo something far older: Indigenous peoples have practised and taught land stewardship across generations. Always think of nature as a best friend and treat it with love and respect.
Learn it. Live it. Pass it on.

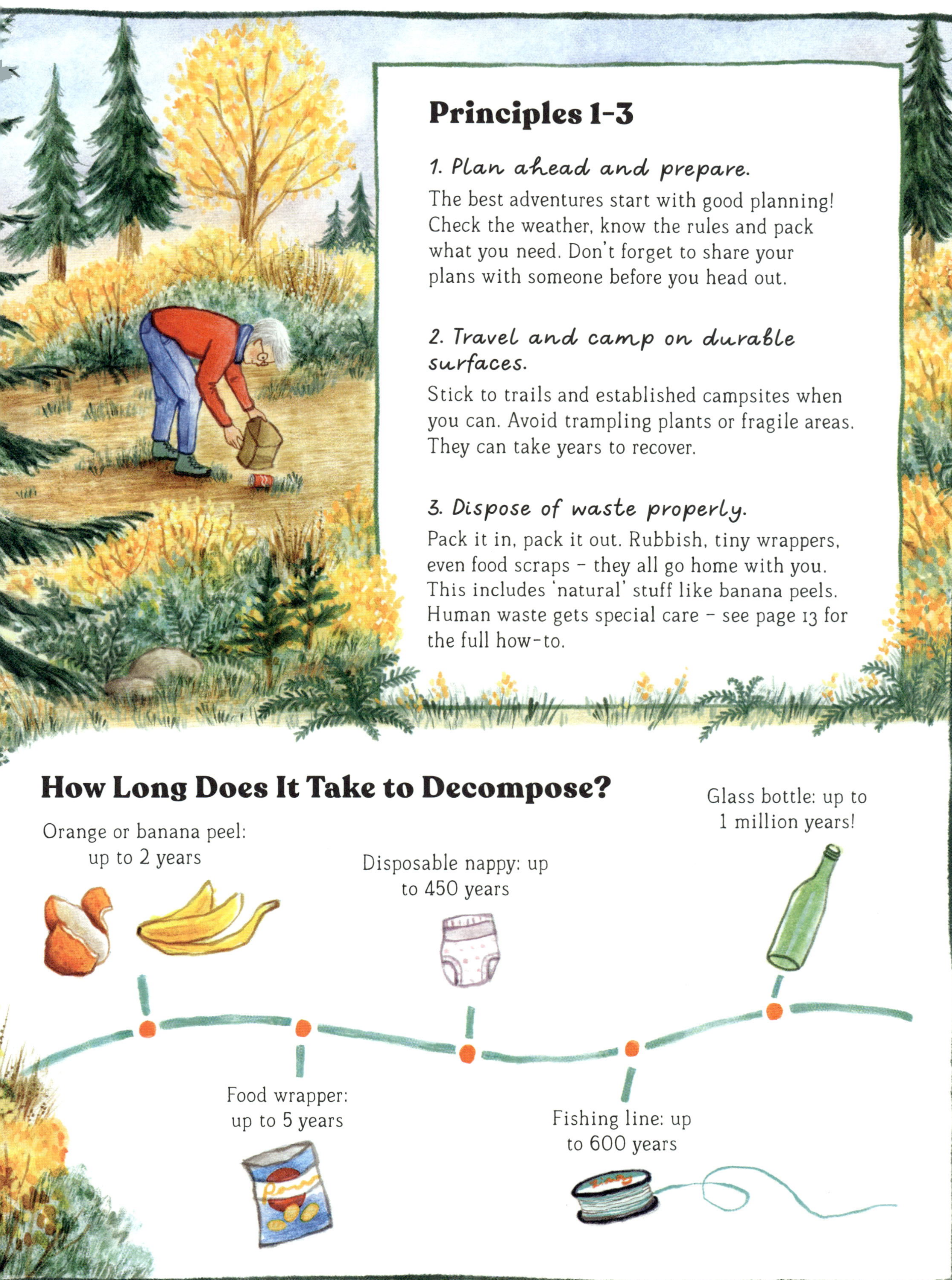

Principles 1-3

1. Plan ahead and prepare.

The best adventures start with good planning! Check the weather, know the rules and pack what you need. Don't forget to share your plans with someone before you head out.

2. Travel and camp on durable surfaces.

Stick to trails and established campsites when you can. Avoid trampling plants or fragile areas. They can take years to recover.

3. Dispose of waste properly.

Pack it in, pack it out. Rubbish, tiny wrappers, even food scraps – they all go home with you. This includes 'natural' stuff like banana peels. Human waste gets special care – see page 13 for the full how-to.

How Long Does It Take to Decompose?

Orange or banana peel: up to 2 years

Food wrapper: up to 5 years

Disposable nappy: up to 450 years

Fishing line: up to 600 years

Glass bottle: up to 1 million years!

Principles 4-6

4. Leave what you find.

Rocks, flowers, feathers – let them stay where nature put them. Take photos instead of souvenirs so the next explorer gets the same wild experience you did.

5. Minimize campfire impacts.

Fires are awesome, but they can scar the land for years. Check if fires are allowed. Keep them small and only in fire rings or existing pits. Never cut live trees, and make sure your fire is completely extinguished before leaving.

6. Respect wildlife.

Watch animals from a distance and give them space to be wild. Stay about 20 metres back from most wildlife and 90 metres back from bigger animals. Never feed them – human food can hurt them and make them rely on people.

Animal Viewing Thumb Trick

It can be tough to judge distance, so here's a technique you can use in the field:

- Arm straight, thumb up; close one eye.
- Try to cover the animal with your thumb.
- If you can't cover it, you're too close – back up.

Principle 7

7. Be considerate of others.

Everyone's out here for their own adventure. Keep noise low, and be courteous to other people you cross paths with. Respect makes the outdoors better for everyone.

Leave It Better Than You Found It

Taking a moment to pick up a small piece of rubbish is sure to bring good karma your way! This is one of my favourite practices.

Tip:

Leaving camp or a break spot? Before you hike on, do a 'spin and scan'. Pick up tiny rubbish and make sure you've got all your essentials, like your water bottle or compass. Make this a habit.

Further Reading Leave No Trace

For up-to-date advice, activities and science, visit lnt.org.

FINDING FORGOTTEN SKILLS . . . OUTDOORS

As screens replaced campfires, something vital was forgotten... the skills that once connected us to the wild. This book helps bring the most essential ones back to light.

Whether you love camping, fishing, building or exploring, there's always another skill waiting to be learned.

Discovery begins with conversation. Ask an older adult you know and trust – a parent, grandparent, teacher or family friend – how they spent time outdoors when they were your age. Watch their eyes light up as those memories return. If something sounds fun, ask if they can show you how it's done. Choose a good place to meet, gather your gear and rediscover the joy together!

Stay curious. Keep practising. You're part of the story that keeps these outdoor skills alive – and our connection to nature strong.

What was your favourite thing to do outdoors when you were my age?

What's your favourite food to eat on an adventure?

What was your favourite wilderness game?

What outdoor skill were you proudest of?

What skill do you think is most important?

What's your all-time favourite outdoor memory?

Do you have any old photos from your adventures I could see?

MORE TO EXPLORE

There are countless outdoor skills still waiting to be discovered. Start with a few of the ideas below. Learning from books and videos is helpful, but the best way is to find an older adult who knows the skill. That's how these skills survive – they are shared, practised and remembered together.

If you liked creating a **BUSHCRAFTER'S TOOLBOX**, *try*

- *Setting up a tarp three different ways*
- *Practising staying warm and dry while hiking in the rain*

If you liked **WHITTLING WOOD**, *try*

- *Carving a hiking stick*
- *Whittling a tent stake*

If you liked **PURIFYING WILD WATER**, *try*

- *Finding water sources in the wild*
- *Collecting rainwater in the wild*

If you liked **SETTING UP CAMP**, *try*

- *Helping to plan a camping trip to a new location*
- *Hanging food from a tree so bears and other animals can't get to it*

If you liked **TELLING TIME WITHOUT A CLOCK**, *try*

- *Making a sundial*
- *Finding north without a compass*

If you liked **IDENTIFYING ANIMAL TRACKS AND SCAT**, *try*

- *Identifying bird sounds*
- *Identifying animal nests*

If you liked **READING A RIVER**, *try*

- *Skipping stones*
- *Identifying three different plants growing on a riverbank*

If you liked **BUILDING A CAMPFIRE**, *try*

- *Using a firesteel*
- *Toasting the perfect marshmallow*

If you liked making a **POCKET FISHING KIT**, *try*

- *Digging your own bait*
- *Fly fishing*

If you liked **BUILDING A NATURAL SHELTER**, *try*

- *Pitching a tent*
- *Building a snow cave*

If you liked **MAKING NATURAL CORDAGE**, *try*

- *Creating fishing line with cordage chain*
- *Making a bow drill*

If you liked **FORAGING**, *try*

- *Making a campfire berry cobbler or crumble*
- *Brewing tea with fresh mint*

If you liked LEARNING WHAT TO DO IF YOU GET LOST, *try*

- *Memorising your parent or caregiver's phone number*
- *Making trail mix to bring on your next hike*

If you liked STARGAZING, *try*

- *Watching a meteor shower*
- *Identifying planets in the night sky*

If you liked COOKING OUTDOORS, *try*

- *Making campfire popcorn*
- *Making a campfire foil packet meal*

If you liked PREDICTING THE WEATHER, *try*

- *Measuring humidity with a pinecone*
- *Figuring out which direction the wind is blowing*

If you liked APPLYING FIRST AID, *try*

- *Learning how to handle wild animal encounters*
- *Taking a first aid course*

If you liked TYING KNOTS, *try*

- *Hanging a hammock*
- *Setting up a clothesline*

If you liked PLAYING WILDERNESS GAMES, *try*

- *Camping Bingo*
- *Setting up an obstacle course*

If you liked LASHING, *try*

- *Tripod lashing*
- *Diagonal lashing*

If you liked USING A COMPASS, *try*

- *A compass scavenger hunt*
- *Following a trail map and using trail markers*

FURTHER READING

Bushcraft Kid: Survive in the Wild and Have Fun Doing It!
by Dan Wowak

Camping Activity Book for Kids: 35 Fun Projects for Your Next Outdoor Adventure
by Amelia Mayer

Exploring Nature Activity Book for Kids: 50 Creative Projects to Spark Curiosity in the Outdoors
by Kim Andrews

Hike It: An Introduction to Camping, Hiking, and Backpacking in the U.S.A.
by Iron Tazz

The Secret Signs of Nature: How to Uncover Hidden Clues in the Sky, Water, Plants, Animals, and Weather
by Craig Caudill

Survivor Kid: A Practical Guide to Wilderness Survival
by Denise Long

The Highlights Book of Things to Do Outdoors: Explore, Unearth, and Build Great Things Outside
by Highlights

You Decide Your Adventure: Join Bear Grylls on the Ultimate Expedition
by Bear Grylls

INDEX